Hannah Arendt

LECTURES ON

KANT'S
Political Philosophy

EDITED AND WITH AN INTERPRETIVE ESSAY BY

Ronald Beiner

THE UNIVERSITY OF CHICAGO PRESS

The University of Chicago Press, Chicago 60637
The Harvester Press, Limited, Brighton, Sussex

©1982 by The University of Chicago
All rights reserved. Published 1982
Paperback edition 1989
Printed in the United States of America
98 97 96 95 94 93 92 91 90   6 5 4 3

Library of Congress Cataloging in Publication Data

Arendt, Hannah.
    Lectures on Kant's political philosophy.

    Includes bibliographical references.
    1. Kant, Immanuel, 1724–1804—Addresses, essays,
lectures.   I. Beiner, Ronald, 1953–
II. Title.
JC181.K4A73   320'.01'0924   82-4817
ISBN 0-226-02594-2   AACR2
ISBN 0-226-02595-0 (pbk.)

Hannah Arendt's "Postscriptum" to *The Life of the
Mind,* volume one, ©1977, 1978 by Harcourt Brace
Jovanovich, Inc., is reprinted with the permission of
the publishers, Harcourt Brace Jovanovich, Inc., and
Martin Secker & Warburg, Limited.

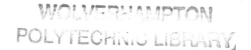

Contents

Preface

HANNAH ARENDT never lived to write "Judging," which was to have been the third and concluding part of her work *The Life of the Mind*. Yet students of her thought would have ample justification for believing that, had it been written, it would have been her crowning achievement. The purpose of the present book is to draw together the main available texts by Arendt on this important topic. Obviously, these texts can be no substitute for the work that was not written, but I think they can offer clues to the likely direction Hannah Arendt's thinking would have taken in this area, especially when they are viewed in the context of her work as a whole. In my interpretive essay I have hoped to show that something coherent can indeed be gleaned from these texts and to help give the reader some sense of their importance. No more than this is claimed for my speculative reconstruction.

The first text is Arendt's *Postscriptum* to volume one of *The Life of the Mind*. This forms a prelude to "Judging," since it offers a brief plan of the projected work and indicates the basic themes and overall intention. (The *Postscriptum*, the last chapter of *Thinking*, forms a transition between the two volumes of *The Life of the Mind*, and announces the main topics intended for treatment in volume two.) The Lectures on Kant's Political Philosophy, the core of the present volume, are an exposition of Kant's aesthetic and political writings, designed to show that the *Critique of Judgment* contains the outlines of a powerful and important *political* philosophy—one that Kant himself did not develop explicitly (and of which he was perhaps not fully conscious) but that may, nonetheless, constitute his greatest legacy to political philosophers. Hannah Arendt gave these Kant Lectures first at the New School for Social Research, during the Fall semester of 1970. She had presented an earlier version of them at the University of Chicago in 1964, and material on judging was also included in

lectures she gave on moral philosophy at Chicago and at the
New School during 1965 and 1966. Arendt was scheduled to
lecture again on the *Critique of Judgment* in the Spring semester
of 1976 at the New School, but her death came in December,
1975. The notes on Imagination are from a seminar on the
Critique of Judgment given at the New School during the same
semester as the 1970 Kant Lectures. (Arendt commonly gave
seminars concurrently with lectures on closely related topics in
order to explore certain ideas in greater depth.) These seminar
notes help to elaborate the Kant Lectures by showing that the
notion of exemplary validity that emerges in the third *Critique*
and the doctrine of the Schematism in the first *Critique* are linked
by the role of imagination, which is fundamental to both, providing schemata for cognition as well as examples for judgment.

My aim has been to provide as full a selection of texts as the
reader would need in order to glimpse Hannah Arendt's
emerging reflections on judging. Other available lecture materials have been left out because to have included them would
have produced either repetitiveness, where her views had not
changed, or inconsistency, where her views had developed beyond those expressed in the earlier sketches. I have, however,
made use of these other materials, where they are relevant, in
my commentary.

The writings assembled in this volume are, in the main, lecture notes that were never intended for publication. Although
changes have been made where the wording or punctuation
seemed ungrammatical or insufficiently clear, the substance has
not been altered, and they retain their original form as notes for
lectures. Thus the contents of this volume should in no way be
mistaken for finished compositions. The reason for their being
made available is simply to give access to ideas of signal
importance—ideas that the author herself did not live to develop
in the way she had intended.

Arendt's citations of sources in the lecture and seminar notes
were often rather sketchy, and some were plainly inaccurate.
The responsibility for the notes accompanying Arendt's texts is,
therefore, entirely mine.

I am deeply indebted to Mary McCarthy for her constant help
and unfailing kindness, without which this volume would not
have been possible. I am obliged also to the staff of the Manuscript Division of the Library of Congress for their helpful cooperation.

PART ONE

Texts by Arendt

Postscriptum to *Thinking*

From *The Life of the Mind,* Volume One

IN THE SECOND VOLUME of this work [*The Life of the Mind*] I shall deal with willing and judging, the two other mental activities. Looked at from the perspective of these time speculations, they concern matters that are absent either because they are not yet or because they are no more; but in contradistinction to the thinking activity, which deals with the invisibles in all experience and always tends to generalize, they always deal with particulars and in this respect are much closer to the world of appearances. If we wish to placate our common sense, so decisively offended by the need of reason to pursue its purposeless quest for meaning, it is tempting to justify this need solely on the grounds that thinking is an indispensable preparation for deciding what shall be and for evaluating what is no more. Since the past, being past, becomes subject to our judgment, judgment, in turn, would be a mere preparation for willing. This is undeniably the perspective, and, within limits, the legitimate perspective, of man insofar as he is an acting being.

But this last attempt to defend the thinking activity against the reproach of being impractical and useless does not work. The decision the will arrives at can never be derived from the mechanics of desire or the deliberations of the intellect that may precede it. The will is either an organ of free spontaneity that interrupts all causal chains of motivation that would bind it or it is nothing but an illusion. In respect to desire, on one hand, and to reason, on the other, the will acts like "a kind of *coup d'état,*" as Bergson once said, and this implies, of course, that "free acts are exceptional": "although we are free whenever we are willing to get back into ourselves, *it seldom happens that we are willing.*"[1] In other words, it is impossible to deal with the willing activity without touching on the problem of freedom.

3

[Three paragraphs of the original text, pertaining to the account of willing in volume two of *The Life of the Mind,* are omitted
here.—R.B.]

I shall conclude the second volume with an analysis of the
faculty of judgment, and here the chief difficulty will be the
curious scarcity of sources providing authoritative testimony.
Not till Kant's *Critique of Judgment* did this faculty become a
major topic of a major thinker.

I shall show that my own main assumption in singling out
judgment as a distinct capacity of our minds has been that judgments are not arrived at by either deduction or induction; in short,
they have nothing in common with logical operations—as when
we say: All men are mortal, Socrates is a man, hence, Socrates is
mortal. We shall be in search of the "silent sense," which—when
it was dealt with at all—has always, even in Kant, been thought of
as "taste" and therefore as belonging to the realm of aesthetics.
In practical and moral matters it was called "conscience," and
conscience did not judge; it told you, as the divine voice of either
God or reason, what to do, what not to do, and what to repent of.
Whatever the voice of conscience may be, it cannot be said to be
"silent," and its validity depends entirely upon an authority that
is above and beyond all merely human laws and rules.

In Kant judgment emerges as "a peculiar talent which can be
practiced only and cannot be taught." Judgment deals with particulars, and when the thinking ego moving among generalities
emerges from its withdrawal and returns to the world of particular appearances, it turns out that the mind needs a new "gift"
to deal with them. "An obtuse or narrow-minded person," Kant
believed, " . . . may indeed be trained through study, even to the
extent of becoming learned. But as such people are commonly
still lacking in judgment, it is not unusual to meet learned men
who in the application of their scientific knowledge betray that
original want, which can never be made good."[2] In Kant, it is
reason with its "regulative ideas" that comes to the help of judgment; but if the faculty is separate from other faculties of the
mind, then we shall have to ascribe to it its own *modus operandi,* its
own way of proceeding.

And this is of some relevance to a whole set of problems by
which modern thought is haunted, especially to the problem of
theory and practice and to all attempts to arrive at a halfway
plausible theory of ethics. Since Hegel and Marx, these questions
have been treated in the perspective of History and on the as-

sumption that there is such a thing as Progress of the human race. Finally we shall be left with the only alternative there is in these matters. Either we can say with Hegel: *Die Weltgeschichte ist das Weltgericht,* leaving the ultimate judgment to Success, or we can maintain with Kant the autonomy of the minds of men and their possible independence of things as they are or as they have come into being.

Here we shall have to concern ourselves, not for the first time,[3] with the concept of history, but we may be able to reflect on the oldest meaning of this word, which, like so many other terms in our political and philosophical language, is Greek in origin, derived from *historein,* "to inquire in order to tell how it was"— *legein ta eonta* in Herodotus. But the origin of this verb is in turn Homer (*Iliad* XVIII), where the noun *histōr* ("historian," as it were) occurs, and that Homeric historian is the *judge.* If judgment is our faculty for dealing with the past, the historian is the inquiring man who by relating it sits in judgment over it. If that is so, we may reclaim our human dignity, win it back, as it were, from the pseudo-divinity named History of the modern age, without denying history's importance but denying its right to be the ultimate judge. Old Cato, with whom I started these reflections—"Never am I less alone than when I am by myself, never am I more active than when I do nothing"—has left us a curious phrase, which aptly sums up the political principle implied in the enterprise of reclamation. He said: "*Victrix causa deis placuit, sed victa Catoni*" ("The victorious cause pleased the gods, but the defeated one pleases Cato").

Lectures on
Kant's Political Philosophy

Delivered at the
New School For Social Research,
Fall, 1970

First Session

TO TALK ABOUT and inquire into Kant's political philosophy has
its difficulties. Unlike so many other philosophers—Plato, Aristotle, Augustine, Thomas, Spinoza, Hegel, and others—he never
wrote a political philosophy. The literature on Kant is enormous, but there are very few books on his political philosophy,
and, of these, there is only one that is worth studying—Hans
Saner's *Kants Weg vom Krieg zum Frieden.*[1] In France there appeared, very recently, a collection of essays devoted to Kant's
political philosophy,[2] some of which are interesting; but even
there you will soon see that the question itself is treated as a
marginal topic as far as Kant himself was concerned. Of all the
books on Kant's philosophy as a whole, it is only Jaspers' treatment that devotes at least a quarter of the space to this particular
subject. (Jaspers, the only disciple Kant ever had; Saner, the
only one Jaspers ever had.) The essays that make up *On History*[3]
or the recent collection called *Kant's Political Writings*[4] cannot
compare in quality and depth with Kant's other writings; they
certainly do not constitute a "Fourth Critique," as one author
called them, eager to claim for them that stature since they happened to be his subject.[5] Kant himself called some of them a
mere "play with ideas" or a "mere pleasure trip."[6] And the ironical tone of *Perpetual Peace,* by far the most important of them,
shows clearly that Kant himself did not take them too seriously.
In a letter to Kiesewetter (October 15, 1795), he calls the treatise
"reveries" (as though he thought of his early fun with Sweden-
borg, his *Dreams of a Ghost-Seer, Elucidated by Dreams of Metaphysics*
[1766]). As far as *The Doctrine of Right* (or of Law) is
concerned—which you will find only in the book edited by Reiss
and which, if you read it, you will probably find rather boring

7

and pedantic—it is difficult not to agree with Schopenhauer, who said about it: "It is as if it were not the work of this great man, but the product of an ordinary common man [*gewöhnlicher Erdensohn*]." The concept of law is of great importance in Kant's practical philosophy, where man is understood as a legislative being; but if we want to study the philosophy of law in general, we certainly shall not turn to Kant but to Pufendorff or Grotius or Montesquieu.

Finally, if you look at the other essays—either in the Reiss book or in the other collection (*On History*), you will see that many of them are concerned with history, so that, at first, it looks almost as though Kant, like so many after him, had substituted a philosophy of history for a political philosophy; but then, Kant's concept of history, though quite important in its own right, is not central to his philosophy, and we would turn to Vico or Hegel and Marx if we wanted to inquire into history. In Kant, history is part of nature; the historical subject is the human species under-stood as part of the creation, though as its final end and crea-tion's crown, so to speak. What matters in history, whose haphazard, contingent melancholy he never forgot, are not the stories, not the historical individuals, nothing that men did of good or evil, but the secret ruse of nature that caused the species to progress and develop all of its potentialities in the succession of generations. The lifespan of man as an individual is too short to develop all human qualities and possibilities; the history of the species is therefore the process in which "all the seeds planted in it by Nature can fully develop and in which the destiny of the race can be fulfilled here on earth."[7] This is "world history," seen in analogy to the organic development of the individual—childhood, adolescence, maturity. Kant is never interested in the past; what interests him is the future of the species. Man is driven from Paradise not because of sin and not by an avenging God but by nature, which releases him from her womb and then drives him from the Garden, the "safe and harmless state of childhood."[8] That is the beginning of history; its process is prog-ress, and the product of this process is sometimes called culture,[9] sometimes freedom ("from the tutelage of nature to the state of freedom");[10] and only once, almost in passing, in a parenthesis, does Kant state that it is a question of bringing about "the high-est end intended for man, namely, sociability [*Geselligkeit*]."[11] (We shall see later the importance of sociability.) Progress itself, the dominant concept of the eighteenth century, is for Kant a rather melancholy notion; he repeatedly stresses its obviously sad implication for the life of the individual.

> If we accept the moral-physical condition of man here in life even on the best terms, that is to say, of a perpetual progression and advance to the highest good which is marked out as his destination, he still cannot . . . unite contentment with the prospect of his condition . . . enduring in an eternal state of change. For the condition in which man now exists remains ever an evil, in comparison to the better condition into which he stands ready to proceed; and the notion of an infinite progression to the ultimate purpose is still simultaneously one prospect in an unending series of evils which . . . do not permit contentment to prevail.[12]

Another way of raising objections to my choice of topic, a somewhat indelicate but by no means entirely unjustified way, is to point out that all of the essays that are usually chosen—and that I too have chosen—date from Kant's last years and that the decrease of his mental faculties, which finally led into senile imbecility, is a matter of fact. To counteract this argument, I have asked you to read the very early *Observations on the Feeling of the Beautiful and Sublime*.[13] To anticipate my own opinion on this matter, which I hope to justify to you in the course of this term: if one knows Kant's work and takes its biographical circumstances into account, it is rather tempting to turn the argument around and to say that Kant became aware of the political *as distinguished from the social*, as part and parcel of man's condition in the world, rather late in life, when he no longer had either the strength or the time to work out his own philosophy on this particular matter. By this I do not mean to say that Kant, because of the shortness of his life, failed to write the "fourth Critique" but rather that the third Critique, the *Critique of Judgment*—which in distinction from the *Critique of Practical Reason* was written spontaneously and not, like the *Critique of Practical Reason,* in answer to critical observations, questions, and provocations—actually should have become the book that otherwise is missing in Kant's great work.

After he had finished the critical business, there were, from his own viewpoint, two questions left, questions that had bothered him all his life and that he had interrupted work on in order first to clear up what he called the "scandal of reason": the fact that "reason contradicts itself"[14] or that *thinking* transcends the limitations of what we can *know* and then gets caught in its own antinomies. We know from Kant's own testimony that the turning point in his life was his discovery (in 1770) of the human mind's cognitive faculties and their limitations, a discovery that took him more than ten years to elaborate and to publish as the *Critique of Pure Reason.* We also know from his letters what this immense labor of so many years signified for his other plans and ideas. He writes, of this "main subject," that it kept back and obstructed like "a dam" all the other matters he had hoped to finish and publish; that it was like "a stone on his way," on which he could proceed only after its removal.[15] And when he returned to his concerns of the precritical period, they had, of course, changed somewhat in the light of what he now knew; but they had not changed beyond recognition, nor could we say that they had lost their urgency for him.

The most important change can be indicated in the following way. Prior to the event of 1770, he had intended to write, and soon publish, the *Metaphysics of Morals,* a work that in fact he wrote and published only thirty years later. But, at this early date, the book was announced under the title Critique of Moral Taste.[16] When Kant finally turned to the third *Critique,* he still called it, to begin with, the Critique of Taste. Thus two things happened: behind taste, a favorite topic of the whole eighteenth century, Kant had discovered an entirely new human faculty, namely, judgment; but, at the same time, he withdrew moral propositions from the competence of this new faculty. In other words: it is now more than taste that will decide about the beautiful and the ugly; but the question of right and wrong is to be decided by neither taste nor judgment but by reason alone.

Second Session

IN THE FIRST LECTURE I said that for Kant, toward the end of his life, two questions were left. The first of these could be summed up, or rather indicated, by the "sociability" of man, that is, the fact that no man can live alone, that men are interdependent not merely in their needs and cares but in their highest faculty, the human mind, which will not function outside human society. "Company is indispensable for the *thinker.*"[17] This concept is a key to the first part of the *Critique of Judgment.* That the *Critique of Judgment,* or of Taste, was written in response to a leftover question from the precritical period is obvious. Like the *Observations,* the *Critique* again is divided into the Beautiful and the Sublime. And in the earlier work, which reads as though it had been written by one of the French moralists, the question of "sociability," of company, was already, though not to the same extent, a key question. Kant there reports the actual experience that lies behind the "problem," and the experience, apart from the actual social life of the young Kant, was a kind of thought-experiment. The experiment goes as follows:

["Carazan's Dream":] In proportion as his riches increased, this wealthy miser had closed off his heart from compassion and love toward all others. Meantime, as the love of man grew cold in him, the diligence of his prayer and his religious observances increased. After this confession, he goes on to recount the following: "One evening, as by my lamp I drew up my accounts and calculated my profits, sleep overpowered me. In this state I saw the Angel of Death come over me like a whirlwind. He struck me before I could plead to be spared his terrible stroke. I was petrified, as I perceived that my destiny throughout eternity was cast, and that to all the good I had done nothing could be added, and from all the evil I had committed, not a thing could be taken away. I was led before the throne of him who dwells in the third heaven. The glory that flamed before me spoke to me thus: 'Carazan, your service of God is rejected. You have closed your heart to the love of man, and have clutched your treasures with an iron grip. You have lived only for yourself, and therefore you shall also live the future in eternity alone and removed from all communion with the whole of Creation.' At this instant I was swept away by an unseen power, and driven through the shining edifice of Creation. I soon left countless worlds behind me. As I neared the outermost end of nature, I saw the shadows of the boundless void sink down into the abyss before me. A fearful kingdom of eternal silence, loneliness, and darkness! Unutterable horror overtook me at this sight. I gradually lost sight of the last star, and finally the last glimmering ray of light was extinguished in outer darkness! The mortal terrors of despair increased with every moment, just as every moment increased my distance from the last inhabited world. I reflected with unbearable anguish that if ten thousand times a thousand years more should have carried me along beyond the bounds of all the universe I would still always be looking ahead into the infinite abyss of darkness, without help or hope of any return.—In this bewilderment I thrust out my hands with such force toward the objects of reality that I awoke. And now I have been taught to esteem mankind; for in that terrifying solitude I would have preferred even the least of those whom in the pride of my fortune I had turned from my door to all the treasures of Golconda."[18]

The second leftover question is central to the *Critique*'s second part, which is so different from the first that the book's lack of unity has always provoked comment; Baeumler, for example, asked if it was anything more than an "old man's whim" (*Greisenschrulle*).[19] This second question, raised in §67 of the *Critique of Judgment,* reads: "Why is it necessary that men should exist at all?" This question, too, is a kind of leftover concern. You all know the famous three questions whose answer, according to Kant, constituted the proper business of philosophy: What can I know? What ought I to do? What may I hope? To these three, he used to add a fourth in his lecture courses: *What is Man?* And he explained: "One could call them all together 'anthropology' because the first three questions relate to [indicate] the last one."[20] This question has an obvious relationship to the other question, asked by Leibniz, by Schelling, by Heidegger: Why should there be anything and not rather nothing? Leibniz calls it "the first question we have a right to raise" and adds: "For nothing is simpler and easier than something."[21] It should be obvious that, however you phrase these why-questions, every answer that would start with Because . . . would sound, and be, only silly. For the why actually does not ask for a *cause,* as, for example, How did life develop, or How came the universe into existence (with or without a bang); rather, it asks for what *purpose* did all this happen, and "the purpose, for instance of the existence of nature, must be sought beyond nature,"[22] the purpose of life beyond life, the purpose of the universe beyond the universe. This purpose, like every purpose, must be more than nature, life, or the universe, which immediately, by this question, are degraded into means for something higher than themselves. (When Heidegger, in his late philosophy, tries time and again to put man and being into a kind of correspondence in which one presupposes and conditions the other—Being calling for Man, Man becoming the guardian or shepherd of Being, Being needing Man for its own appearance, Man not just needing Being in order to exist at all but being concerned with his own Being as no other entity [*Seiendes:* being], no other living thing, is,[23] etc.—it is to escape this kind of mutual degradation, inher-

ent in these general why-questions, rather than to escape the
paradoxes of all thoughts about Nothingness.)

Kant's own answer to this perplexity, as derived from the second part of the *Critique of Judgment,* would have been: We ask
such questions as What is the purpose of nature? only because
we ourselves are purposive beings who constantly design aims
and ends and belong, as such intentional beings, to nature. In
the same vein, one could answer the question why we perplex
ourselves with such obviously unanswerable questions as Does
the world or the universe have a beginning, or is it, like God
himself, from eternity to eternity? by pointing to the fact that it is
in our very nature to be beginners and hence to constitute beginnings throughout our lives.[24]

But to come back to the *Critique of Judgment:* The links between
its two parts are weak, but, such as they are—i.e., as they can be
assumed to have existed in Kant's own mind—they are more
closely connected with the political than with anything in the
other *Critiques.* There are two important links. The first is that in
neither of the two parts does Kant speak of man as an intelligible
or a cognitive being. The word truth does not occur—except
once, in a special context. The first part speaks of men in the
plural, as they really are and live in societies; the second part
speaks of the human species. (Kant underlines this in the passage I have just quoted by adding: the question "why it is necessary that men should exist . . . we shall not find so easy to answer
if we sometimes cast our thoughts on the New Hollanders or
[other primitive tribes].")[25] The most decisive difference between the *Critique of Practical Reason* and the *Critique of Judgment*
is that the moral laws of the former are valid for all intelligible
beings, whereas the rules of the latter are strictly limited in their
validity to human beings on earth. The second link lies in the
fact that the faculty of judgment deals with particulars, which "as
such, contain something contingent in respect of the universal,"[26] which normally is what thought is dealing with. These
particulars are again of two kinds; the first part of the *Critique of
Judgment* deals wth objects of judgment properly speaking, such
as an object that we call "beautiful" without being able to subsume it under a general category of Beauty as such; we have no
rule that could be applied. (If you say, "What a beautiful rose!"
you do not arrive at this judgment by first saying, "All roses are
beautiful, this flower is a rose, hence this rose is beautiful." Or,
conversely, "Beauty is roses, this flower is a rose, hence, it is

beautiful.") The other kind, dealt with in the second part of the *Critique of Judgment* is the impossibility of deriving any particular product of nature from general causes: "Absolutely no human reason (in fact, no finite reason like ours in quality, however much it may surpass it in degree) can hope to understand the production of even a blade of grass by mere mechanical causes."[27] ("Mechanical" in Kant's terminology refers to natural causes; its opposite is "technical," by which he means "artificial," i.e., something fabricated with a purpose. The distinction is between things that come into being of themselves and those that are fabricated for a specific end or purpose.) The accent here is on "understand": How can I understand (and not just explain) that there is grass at all and then this particular blade of grass? Kant's solution is to introduce the teleological principle, "the principle of purposes in the products of nature," as a "heuristic principle for investigating the particular laws of nature," which, however, does not make "their mode of origination any more comprehensible."[28] We are not concerned here with this part of Kant's philosophy; it does not deal with judgment of the particular, strictly speaking, and its topic is nature, although, as we shall see, Kant understands history also as part of nature—it is the history of the human species insofar as it belongs to the animal species on earth. Its intention is to find a principle of cognition rather than a principle of judgment. But you should see that just as you can raise the question Why is it necessary that men should exist at all? you can continue and ask why it is necessary that trees should exist, or blades of grass, and so on.

In other words, the topics of the *Critique of Judgment*—the particular, whether a fact of nature or an event in history; the faculty of judgment as the faculty of man's mind to deal with it; sociability of men as the condition of the functioning of this faculty, that is, the insight that men are dependent on their fellow men not only because of their having a body and physical needs but precisely for their mental faculties—these topics, all of them of eminent political significance—that is, important for the political—were concerns of Kant long before he finally, after finishing the critical business (*das kritische Geschäft*), turned to them when he was old. And it was for their sake that he postponed the doctrinal part, to which he had intended to proceed "in order to profit, as far as is possible, by the more favorable moments of my increasing years."[29] This doctrinal part was supposed to contain "the metaphysics of nature and of morals";

there would be no place in them, "no special section, for the faculty of judgment." For judgment of the particular—*This* is beautiful, *This* is ugly; This is right, This is wrong—has no place in Kant's moral philosophy. Judgment is not practical reason; practical reason "reasons" and tells me what to do and what not to do; it lays down the law and is identical with the will, and the will utters commands; it speaks in imperatives. Judgment, on the contrary, arises from "a merely contemplative pleasure or inactive delight [*untätiges Wohlgefallen*]."[30]

This "feeling of contemplative pleasure is called taste," and the *Critique of Judgment* was originally called Critique of Taste. "If practical philosophy speaks of contemplative pleasure at all, it mentions it only in passing, and not as if the concept were indigenous to it."[31] Does that not sound plausible? How could "contemplative pleasure and inactive delight" have anything to do with practice? Does that not conclusively prove that Kant, when he turned to the doctrinal business, had decided that his concern with the particular and contingent was a thing of the past and had been a somewhat marginal affair? And yet, we shall see that his final position on the French Revolution, an event that played a central role in his old age, when he waited with great impatience every day for the newspapers, was decided by this attitude of the mere spectator, of those "who are not engaged in the game themselves" but only follow it with "wishful, passionate participation," which certainly did not mean, least of all for Kant, that they now wanted to make a revolution; their sympathy arose from mere "contemplative pleasure and inactive delight."

There is only one element in Kant's late writings on these subjects that we cannot trace to concerns of the precritical period. Nowhere in the earlier period do we find him interested in strictly constitutional and institutional questions. Yet this interest was paramount in the last years of his life, when nearly all of his strictly political essays were written. These were written after 1790, when the *Critique of Judgment* appeared, and, more significantly, after 1789, the year of the French Revolution, when he was sixty-five years old. From then on his interest no longer turned exclusively about the particular, about history, about human sociability. In its center was rather what we today would call constitutional law—the way a body politic should be organized and constituted, the concept of "republican," i.e., constitutional government, the question of international relations, etc. The first indication of this change is perhaps to be found in the note to § 65 of the *Critique of Judgment,* which relates to the American Revolution, in which Kant had already been very interested. He writes:

> In a recent complete transformation of a great people into a state the word *organization* for the regulation of magistracies, etc., and even of the whole body politic, has often been fitly used. For in such a whole every member should surely be purpose as well as means, and, whilst all work together towards the possibility of the whole, each should be determined as regards place and function by means of the Idea of the whole.

It is precisely this problem of how to organize a people into a state, how to constitute the state, how to *found* a commonwealth, and all the legal problems connected with these questions, that occupied him constantly during his last years. Not that the older concerns with the ruse of nature or with the mere sociability of men had disappeared altogether. But they undergo a certain change or, rather, appear in new and unexpected formulations. Thus we find the curious Article in *Perpetual Peace* that establishes a *Besuchsrecht,* the right to visit foreign lands, the right to hospitality, and "the right of temporary sojourn."[32] And, in the same treatise, we again find nature, that great artist, as the eventual "guarantee of perpetual peace."[33] But without this new preoccupation, it seems rather unlikely that he would have started his *Metaphysics of Morals* with the "Doctrine of Law." Nor is it likely that he would finally have said (in the second section of *The Strife of the Faculties,* the last section of which already shows clear evidence of his mind's deterioration): "It is so sweet to plan state constitutions [*Es ist so süss sich Staatsverfassungen auszudenken*]"—a "sweet dream" whose consummation is "not only thinkable but . . . an obligation, not [however] of the citizens but of the sovereign."[34]

Third Session

ONE WOULD THINK that Kant's problem at this late time in his life—when the American and, even more, the French Revolution had awakened him, so to speak, from his political slumber (as Hume had awakened him in his youth from dogmatic

slumber, and Rousseau had roused him in his manhood from
moral slumber)—was how to reconcile the problem of the or-
ganization of the state with his moral philosophy, that is, with the
dictate of practical reason. And the surprising fact is that he
knew that his moral philosophy could not help here. Thus he
kept away from all moralizing and understood that the problem
was how to force man "to be a good citizen even if [he is] not a
morally good person" and that "a good constitution is not to be
expected from morality, but, conversely, a good moral condition
of a people is to be expected under a good constitution."[35] This
may remind you of Aristotle's remark that a "good man can be a
good citizen only in a good state," except that Kant concludes (and
this is so surprising and goes far beyond Aristotle in separating
morality from good citizenship):

> The problem of organizing a state, however hard it may seem,
> can be solved even for a race of devils, if only they are in-
> telligent. The problem is: "Given a multitude of rational be-
> ings requiring universal laws for their preservation, but each
> of whom is secretly inclined to exempt himself from them, to
> establish a constitution in such a way that, although their pri-
> vate intentions conflict, they check each other, with the result
> that their public conduct is the same as if they had no such
> intentions."[36]

This passage is crucial. What Kant said is—to vary the Aristotelian formula—that a bad man can be a good citizen in a good
state. His definition of "bad" here is in accordance with his moral
philosophy. The categorical imperative tells you: Always act in
such a way that the maxim of your acts can become a general
law, that is, "I am never to act otherwise than so that I could also
will that my maxim should become a universal law."[37] The point
of the matter is very simple. In Kant's own words: I can will a
particular lie, but I "can by no means will that lying should be the
universal law. For with such a law there would be no promises at
all."[38] Or: I can want to steal, but I cannot will stealing to be a universal law; because, with such a law, there would be no property.
The bad man is, for Kant, the one who makes an exception for
himself; he is *not* the man who wills evil, for this, according to
Kant, is impossible. Hence the "race of devils" here are not devils
in the usual sense but those who are "secretly inclined to
exempt" themselves. The point is *secretly:* they could not do it
publicly because then they would obviously stand against the
common interest—be enemies of the people, even if these

people were a race of devils. And in politics, as distinguished from morals, everything depends on "*public* conduct."

Hence, it might appear that this passage could have been written only *after* the *Critique of Practical Reason.* But this is an error. For this, too, is a leftover thought from the precritical period; only now it is formulated in terms of Kant's moral philosophy. In the *Observations on the Feeling of the Beautiful and Sublime* we read:

> Among men there are but few who behave according to *principles*—which is extremely good, as it can so easily happen that one errs in these principles. . . . Those who act out of *goodhearted impulses* are far more numerous [than those acting on the basis of principles]. . . . [However,] those other instincts that so regularly control the animal world . . . perform the great purpose of nature just as well. . . . [And] most men . . . have their best-loved selves fixed before their eyes as the only point of reference for their exertions, and . . . seek to turn everything around *self-interest* as around the great axis. Nothing can be more advantageous than this, for these are the most diligent, orderly, and prudent; they give support and solidity to the whole, while without intending to do so they serve the common good.[39]

Here it even sounds as though "a race of devils" is necessary to "provide the necessary requirements and supply the foundations over which finer souls can spread beauty and harmony."[40] We have here the Kantian version of the theory of enlightened self-interest. This theory has very important shortcomings. But the main points in Kant's position, as far as political philosophy is concerned, are the following. First, it is clear that this scheme can work only if one assumes a "great purpose of nature" working behind the backs of acting men. Otherwise, the race of devils would destroy themselves (in Kant, evil is generally self-destructive). Nature wants the preservation of the species, and all it demands of its children is that they be self-preserving and have brains. Second, there is the conviction that no moral conversion of man, no revolution in his mentality, is needed, required, or hoped for in order to bring about political change for the better. And third, there is the stress on constitutions, on the one hand, and on *publicity,* on the other. "Publicity" is one of the key concepts of Kant's political thinking; in this context, it indicates his conviction that evil thoughts are secret by definition. Thus we read, in one of his late works, *The Strife of the Faculties:*

Why has a ruler never dared openly to declare that he recognizes absolutely no right of the people opposed to him . . . ? The reason is that such a public declaration would rouse all of his subjects against him; although, as docile sheep, led by a benevolent and sensible master, well-fed and powerfully protected, they would have nothing wanting in their welfare for which to lament.[41]

Against all of the justifications I have offered for choosing to discuss a Kantian topic that, literally speaking, is nonexistent—i.e., his nonwritten political philosophy—there exists one objection that we shall never be able to overcome altogether. Kant repeatedly formulated what he held to be the three central questions that make men philosophize and to which his own philosophy tried to give an answer, and none of these questions concerns man as a *zōon politikon,* a political being. Of these questions—What can I know? What ought I to do? What may I hope?—two deal with the traditional topics of metaphysics, God and immortality. It would be a serious error to believe that the second question—What ought I to do?—and its correlate, the idea of freedom, could in any way be relied on to help us in our inquiry. (On the contrary, we shall see that the way Kant phrased the question and answered it will be in our way—and probably was in Kant's own way, too, when he tried to reconcile his political insights with his moral philosophy—when we try to suggest what Kant's political philosophy would have been like had he found the time and the strength to express it adequately.) The second question does not deal with action at all, and Kant nowhere takes action into account. He spelled out man's basic "sociability" and enumerated as elements of it communicability, the need of men to communicate, and publicity, the *public* freedom not just to think but to publish—the "freedom of the pen"; but he does not know either a faculty or a need for *action.* Thus in Kant the question What ought I to do? concerns the conduct of the self in its independence of others—the same self that wants to know what is knowable for human beings and what remains unknowable but is still thinkable, the same self that wants to know what it may reasonably hope for in matters of immortality. The three questions are interconnected in a basically very simple, almost primitive, way. The answer to the first question, given in the *Critique of Pure Reason,* tells me what I can and—what is more important in the last analysis—what I cannot know. Metaphysical questions in Kant deal precisely with what I cannot know. Still, I cannot help thinking about what I cannot know, because it concerns what I am most interested in: the existence of God; freedom, without which life would be undignified for man, would be "beastly"; and the immortality of the soul. In Kant's terminology, these are practical questions, and it is practical reason that tells me how to think about them. Even religion exists for men as rational beings "within the limits of Reason alone." My main interest, what I wish to hope for, is felicity in a future life; and for this I may hope, if I am worthy of it—that is, if I conduct myself in the right manner. In one of his lecture courses and also in his reflections, Kant adds a fourth question to the three, which is meant to sum them up. This is the question What is Man? But this last question does not appear in the *Critiques.*

Moreover, since the question How do I judge?—the question of the third *Critique*—is also absent, none of the basically philosophical questions even so much as mentions the condition of human plurality—except, of course, for what is implicit in the second question: that without other men there would be not much point in conducting myself. But Kant's insistence on the duties toward myself, his insistence that moral duties ought to be free of all inclination and that the moral law should be valid not only for men on this planet but for all intelligible beings in the universe, restricts this condition of plurality to a minimum. The notion underlying all three questions is self-interest, not interest in the world; and while Kant wholeheartedly agreed with the old Roman adage, *Omnes homines beati esse volunt* (All men desire happiness), he felt that he would not be able to stand happiness unless he was also convinced that he was worthy of it. In other words—and these are words repeated many times by Kant, though usually as asides—the greatest misfortune that can befall a man is self-contempt. "The loss of self-approval [*Selbstbilligung*]," he writes in a letter to Mendelssohn (April 8, 1766), "would be the greatest evil that could ever happen to me," not loss of the esteem in which he was held by any other person. (Think of Socrates' statement "It would be better for me to be at odds with the multitudes than, being one, out of harmony with myself.") Hence, the highest goal of the individual in this life is worthiness of a felicity that is unattainable on this earth. Compared to this ultimate concern, all other goals and aims that men may pursue in this life—including, of course, the in any case

dubious progress of the species, which nature works out behind
our backs—are marginal affairs.

At this point, however, we are bound to mention at least the
curiously difficult problem of the relationship between politics
and philosophy or, rather, the attitude philosophers are likely to
have toward the whole political realm. To be sure, other philosophers did what Kant did not do: they wrote political
philosophies; but this does not mean that they therefore had a
higher opinion of it or that political concerns were more central
to their philosophy. The examples are too numerous even to
begin to quote. But Plato clearly wrote the *Republic* to justify the
notion that philosophers should become kings, not because they
would enjoy politics, but because, first, this would mean that they
would not be ruled by people worse than they were themselves
and, second, it would bring about in the commonwealth that complete quiet, that absolute peace, that certainly constitutes the best
condition for the life of the philosopher. Aristotle did not follow
Plato, but even he held that the *bios politikos* in the last analysis
was there for the sake of the *bios theōrētikos;* and, as far as the
philosopher himself was concerned, he said explicitly, even in
the *Politics,* that only philosophy permits men *di' hautōn chairein,*
to enjoy themselves independently, without the help or presence
of others,⁴² whereby it was self-understood that such independence, or rather self-sufficiency, was among the greatest goods.
(To be sure, according to Aristotle, only an active life can assure
happiness; but such "action" "need not be . . . a life which involves relations to others" if it consists in "thoughts and trains of
reflections" that are independent and complete in themselves.)⁴³
Spinoza said in the very title of one of his political treatises that
his ultimate aim in it was not political but the *libertas
philosophandi;* and even Hobbes, who certainly was closer to
political concerns than any other author of a political philosophy
(and neither Machiavelli nor Bodin nor Montesquieu can be said
to have been concerned with philosophy), wrote his *Leviathan* in
order to ward off the dangers of politics and to assure as much
peace and tranquillity as was humanly possible. All of them, with
the possible exception of Hobbes, would have agreed with Plato:
Do not take this whole realm of human affairs too seriously. And
Pascal's words on these matters, written in the vein of French
moralists, hence irreverent, fresh in both meanings of the word,
and sarcastic, may have exaggerated the matter a bit but did not
miss the mark:

We can only think of Plato and Aristotle in grand academic robes. They were honest men, like others, laughing with their friends, and when they wanted to divert themselves, they wrote the *Laws* or the *Politics,* to amuse themselves. That part of their life was the least philosophic and the least serious. The most philosophic [thing] was to live simply and quietly. If they wrote on politics, it was as if laying down rules for a lunatic asylum; if they presented the appearance of speaking of great matters, it was because they knew that the madmen, to whom they spoke, thought they were kings and emperors. They entered into their principles in order to make their madness as little harmful as possible.[44]

Fourth Session

I READ TO YOU a "thought" of Pascal in order to draw your attention to the *relation* between philosophy and politics or, rather, to the attitude nearly all philosophers have had toward the realm of human affairs (*ta tōn anthrōpōn pragmata*). Robert Cumming recently wrote: "The subject-matter of modern political philosophy ... is not the polis or its politics, but the relation between philosophy and politics."[45] This remark actually applies to all political philosophy and, most of all, to its beginnings in Athens.

If we consider Kant's relation to politics from this general perspective—that is, not attributing to him alone what is a general characteristic, a *déformation professionnelle*—we shall find certain agreements and certain very important divergences. The main and most striking agreement is in the attitude toward life and death. You will remember that Plato said that only his body still inhabited the City and, in the *Phaedo,* also explained how right ordinary people are when they say that a philosopher's life is like dying.[46] Death, being the separation of body and soul, is welcome to him; he is somehow in love with death, because the body, with all its demands, constantly interrupts the soul's pursuits.[47] In other words, the true philosopher does not accept the conditions under which life has been given to man. This is not just a whim of Plato, and not just his hostility to the body. It is implicit in Parmenides' trip to the heavens to escape "the opinions of mortals" and the delusions of sense experience, and it is implicit in Heraclitus' withdrawal from his fellow citizens and in those who, asked about their true home, pointed toward the skies; that is, it is implicit in the beginnings of philosophy in

Ionia. And if, with the Romans, we understand being alive as synonymous with *inter homines esse* (and *sinere inter homines esse* as being dead), then we have the first important clue to the sectarian tendencies in philosophy since the time of Pythagoras: withdrawal into a sect is the second-best cure for being alive at all and having to live among men. Most surprisingly, we find a similar position in Socrates, who, after all, brought philosophy down from the heavens to earth; in the *Apology*, likening death to a dreamless sleep, he states that even the great king of Persia would find it difficult to remember many days or nights he had spent better or more pleasantly than a single night in which his sleep was undisturbed by dreams.[48]

To estimate these testimonies of Greek philosophers involves a difficulty. They must be seen against the general Greek pessimism that survives in Sophocles' famous lines: "Not to be born prevails over all meaning uttered in words; by far the second-best thing is for life, once it has appeared, to go back as quickly as possible whence it came" (*Mē phunai ton hapanta nika logon; to d', epei phanē, bēnai keis' hopothen per hēkei polu deuteron hōs tachista* [*Oedipus at Colonus*, 1224–26]). This feeling about life disappeared with the Greeks; what did not disappear but, on the contrary, had the greatest possible influence on the later tradition, was the estimate of what philosophy was all about—no matter whether the authors still spoke out of a specifically Greek experience or out of the specific experience of the philosopher. There is hardly any book that had greater influence than Plato's *Phaedo*. The common Roman and late-antiquity notion that philosophy teaches men first of all how to die is its vulgarized version. (This is un-Greek: in Rome, philosophy, imported from Greece, was a concern of the old; in Greece, on the contrary, it was for the young.) The point for us here is that this preference for death became a general topic of philosophers after Plato. When (in the third century) Zeno, the founder of Stoicism, asked the Delphic Oracle what he should do to attain the best life, the Oracle answered, "Take on the color of the dead." This, as usual, was ambiguous; it could mean, "Live as though you were dead" or, as Zeno himself allegedly interpreted it, "Study the ancients." (Since the anecdote comes to us from Diogenes Laertius [*Lives of the Philosophers* 7. 21], who lived in the third century A.D., both the words of the Delphic Oracle and Zeno's interpretation are uncertain.)

This outspoken suspicion of life could not survive in all its recklessness in the Christian era, for reasons that do not concern us here; you will find it in a characteristic transformation in the theodicies of the modern age, that is, in the justifications of God, behind which there lurks, of course, the suspicion that life as we know it stands in great need of being justified. That this suspicion of life implies a degradation of the whole realm of human affairs, "its melancholy haphazardness" (Kant), is obvious. And the point here is not that life on earth is not immortal but that it is, as the Greeks would say, not "easy," like the life of the gods, but troublesome, full of worries, cares, griefs, and sorrows, and that the pains and displeasures always outweigh the pleasures and gratifications.

Against this background of general pessimism, it is of some importance to understand that the philosophers did not complain about life's mortality or its shortness. Kant even mentions this explicitly: a "greater length would merely prolong a game of unceasing war with troubles."[49] Nor would the species profit if "men could look forward to a life of eight hundred or more years"; for its vices, "endowed with so long a life, would reach a degree where it would deserve no better fate than to be wiped from the face of the earth." This, of course, is in contradiction to the hope for progress in the species, which is constantly being interrupted through the dying of the old members and the birth of new ones, who must spend a very long time learning what the old ones knew already and could have developed further had they been granted a longer lifespan.

Hence, it is life itself whose value is at stake, and in this respect there is hardly any postclassical philosopher who agreed with the Greek philosophers on this point to the same extent as Kant did (albeit without knowing it).

> The value of life for us, if it is estimated by that *which we enjoy* [that is, by happiness], is easy to decide. It sinks below zero; for who would be willing to enter upon life anew under the same conditions? Who would do so even according to a new, self-chosen plan (yet in conformity with the course of nature), if it were merely directed to enjoyment?[50]

Or, with respect to theodicies:

> [If the justification of divine goodness consists] in showing that in the destinies of men evils do not outweigh the pleasant enjoyment of life, since everybody, no matter how badly off he is, prefers life to death, . . . one can leave an answer to this

sophistry to the good sense of each man who has lived long
enough and reflected on the value of life; you have only to ask
him whether he would be willing to play the game of life once
more, not under the same conditions, but under any conditions of our earthly world and not those of some fairy-
land.[51]

In the same essay, Kant calls life a "time of probation" in
which even the best man "will fret his life away" (*seines Lebens nicht
froh wird*), and he speaks in the *Anthropology* of the "burden
which seems to lie on life as such."[52] And, should you think
that—because the stress is on enjoyment, pleasure and pain, and
happiness—this is a small matter for Kant, as a person as well as
a philosopher, he once wrote in the numerous reflections he left
behind (which have been published only in this century) that
only pleasure and displeasure (*Lust* and *Unlust*) "constitute the
absolute, because they are life itself."[53] But you can also read in
the *Critique of Pure Reason* that reason "finds itself constrained to
assume" a future life in which "worthiness and happiness" are
properly connected; "otherwise it would have to regard the
moral laws as empty figments of the brain [*leere Hirngespinste*]."[54]
If the answer to the question What may I hope? is Life in a
future world, the stress is less on immortality than on a better
kind of life.

We now look first into Kant's own philosophy to find out with
what thoughts he might have been able to overcome this deep-
rooted melancholy disposition. For that this was his own case is
beyond doubt, and he himself knew it well. The following de-
scription of "the man of melancholy frame of mind" is certainly
a self-portrait. This man

> cares little for what others judge, what they consider good or
> true [*Selbstdenken*] . . . Truthfulness is sublime, and he hates
> lies or dissimulation. He has a high feeling of the dignity of
> human nature. He values himself and regards a human being
> as a creature who merits respect. He suffers no depraved
> submissiveness, and breathes freedom in a noble breast. All
> chains, from the gilded ones worn at court to the heavy irons
> of galley slaves, are abominable to him. He is a strict judge of
> himself and others, and not seldom is weary of himself as of
> the world. . . . He is in danger of becoming a visionary or a
> crank.[55]

In our inquiry, we should not forget, however, that Kant shared
his general estimate of life with philosophers with whom he

shared neither doctrines nor this specific melancholy.

Two specifically Kantian thoughts come to mind. The first thought is contained in what the Age of Enlightenment called progress, about which we have already spoken. Progress is the progress of the species and is thus of little avail to the individual. But the thought of progress in history as a whole, and for mankind as a whole, implies disregard of the particular and directing one's attention, rather, to the "universal" (as one finds it in the very title of the "Idea of a *Universal* [General] History") in whose context the particular makes sense—to the whole for the existence of which the particular is necessary. This escape, as it were, from the particular, which is in itself meaningless, to the universal, from which it derives its meaning, is of course not peculiar to Kant. The greatest thinker in this respect is Spinoza, with his acquiescence in everything that is—his *amor fati*. But in Kant, also, you will find repeatedly the notion of how necessary war, catastrophes, and plain evil or pain are for the production of "culture." Without them, men would sink back into the brute state of mere animal satisfaction.

The second thought is Kant's notion of the moral dignity of man as an individual. I mentioned earlier the Kantian question Why do men exist at all? This question, according to Kant, can be asked only if one considers the human species as though it were on the same level (and in a certain sense it *is* on the same level) as other animal species. "Of man (and so of every rational creature in the world [i.e., in the universe, not just on earth]) *as a moral being* it can no longer be asked why (*quem in finem*) [to what end] he exists,"[56] for he is an end in himself.

We now have three very different concepts of, or perspectives under which we can consider, the affairs of men: we have the human species and its progress; we have man as a moral being and an end in himself; and we have men in the plural, who actually are in the center of our considerations and whose true "end" is, as I mentioned before, *sociability*. The distinctions among these three perspectives are a necessary precondition for an understanding of Kant. Whenever he speaks of man, one must know whether he is speaking of the human species; or of the moral being, the rational creature that may also exist in other parts of the universe; or of men as actual inhabitants of the earth.

To summarize: Human species = Mankind = part of nature = subject to "history," nature's ruse = to be considered under the idea of "end," teleological judgment: second part of *Critique of Judgment.*

Man = reasonable being, subject to the laws of practical reason which he gives to himself, autonomous, an end in himself, belonging to a *Geisterreich*, realm of intelligible beings = *Critique of Practical Reason* and *Critique of Pure Reason.*

Men = earthbound creatures, living in communities, endowed with common sense, *sensus communis*, a community sense; not autonomous, needing each other's company even for thinking ("freedom of the pen") = first part of the *Critique of Judgment:* aesthetic judgment.

Fifth Session

I SAID THAT I would point out how Kant's attitude as a philosopher toward the realm of human affairs coincides with and diverges from the attitudes of other philosophers, especially Plato. For the moment we shall restrict ourselves to this main point: the attitude of philosophers toward life itself as it is given to men on earth. If you think back to the *Phaedo* and to the motivation given there for the philosopher's being somehow in love with death, you will recall that, though Plato despises the pleasures of the body, he does not complain that the displeasures outweigh the pleasures. The point is rather that pleasures, like displeasures, distract the mind and lead it astray, that the body is a burden if you are after truth, which, being immaterial and beyond sense perception, can be perceived only by the eyes of the soul, which also is immaterial and beyond sense perception. In other words, true cognition is possible only to a mind untroubled by the senses.

This, of course, cannot be Kant's position, for his theoretical philosophy holds that all cognition depends on the interplay and cooperation of sensibility and intellect, and his *Critique of Pure Reason* has rightly been called a justification, if not a glorification, of human sensibility. Even in his youth—when, still under the impact of tradition, he expressed a certain Platonic hostility to the body (he complained that it interfered with the swiftness of thought [*Hurtigkeit des Gedankens*], thus limiting and hindering the mind)[57]—he did not claim that the body and the senses were the chief source of error and evil.

Practically speaking, this has two important consequences.

First, for Kant, the philosopher clarifies the experiences we all have; he does not claim that the philosopher can leave the Platonic Cave or join in Parmenides' journey to the heavens, nor does he think that he should become a member of a sect. For Kant, the philosopher remains a man like you and me, living among his fellow men, *not* among his fellow philosophers. Second, the task of evaluating life with respect to pleasure and displeasure—which Plato and the others claimed for the philosopher alone, holding that the many are quite satisfied with life as it is—Kant claims can be expected from every ordinary man of good sense who ever reflected on life at all.

These two consequences, in turn, are obviously but two sides of the same coin, and the name of the coin is Equality. Let us consider three famous passages from Kant's works. The first two are from the *Critique of Pure Reason,* answering some objections:

> Do you really require that a kind of knowledge which concerns all men should transcend the common understanding, and should only be revealed to you by philosophers? . . . . [In] matters which concern all men without distinction nature is not guilty of any partial distribution of her gifts, and . . . in regard to the essential ends of human nature the highest philosophy cannot advance further than is possible under the guidance which nature has bestowed even upon the most ordinary understanding.[58]

Together with this, consider the very last paragraph of the *Critique:*

> If the reader has had the courtesy and patience to accompany me along this path, he may now judge for himself whether, if he cares to lend his aid in making *this path into a high-road,* it may not be possible to achieve before the end of the present century what many centuries have not been able to accomplish; namely, to secure for human reason complete satisfaction in regard to that with which it has all along so eagerly occupied itself, though hitherto in vain.[59]

The third passage, much quoted, is autobiographical:

> By inclination I am an inquirer. I feel a consuming thirst for knowledge, the unrest which goes with desire to progress in it, and satisfaction in every advance in it. There was a time when I believed this constituted the honor of humanity, and I despised [the] people, who know nothing. Rousseau has put me right [*hat mich zurecht gebracht*]. This blinding prejudice dis-

appeared, and I learned to honor man. I would find myself
more useless than the common laborer if I did not believe that
[what I am doing] can give worth to all others in establishing
the rights of mankind.[60]

Philosophizing, or the thinking of reason, which transcends the
limitations of what can be known, the boundaries of human
cognition, is for Kant a general human "need," the need of
reason as a human faculty. It does not oppose the few to the
many. (If there is a distinctive line between the few and the many
in Kant it is much rather a question of morality: the "foul spot"
in the human species is lying, interpreted as a kind of self-
deception. The "few" are those who are honest with themselves.)
With the disappearance of this age-old distinction, however,
something curious happens. The philosopher's preoccupation
with politics disappears; he no longer has any special interest in
politics; there is no self-interest and hence no claim to either
power or to a constitution that would protect the philosopher
against the many. He agrees with Aristotle, against Plato, that
the philosophers should not rule but that rulers should be willing to listen to the philosophers.[61] But he disagrees with Aristotle's view that the philosophical way of life is the highest and that
the political way of life, in the last analysis, exists for the sake of
the *bios theōrētikos*. With the abandonment of this hierarchy,
which is the abandonment of all hierarchical structures, the old
tension between politics and philosophy disappears altogether.
The result is that politics, and the necessity to write a political
philosophy to lay down the rules for an "insane asylum," ceases
to be an urgent business for the philosopher. It is, in the words
of Eric Weil, no longer "*une préoccupation pour les philosophes; elle
devient, ensemble avec l'histoire, un problème philosophique*" [it is no
longer merely "a source of anxiety for the philosophers; it becomes, together with history, a genuine philosophical problem"].[62]

Moreover, when Kant speaks of the burden that seems to lie
on life itself, he alludes to the curious nature of pleasure, which
Plato, in a different context talks about too; namely, the fact that
all pleasure dispels a displeasure, that a life that contained only
pleasures would actually lack all pleasure—for man would be
unable to feel it or enjoy it—and that, therefore, an entirely pure
delight, untroubled by either the remembrance of the want that
preceded it or the fear of the loss that will certainly succeed it,
does not exist. Happiness as a solid, stable state of soul and body

is unthinkable for men on earth. The greater the want and the greater the displeasure, the more intense will be the pleasure. There is only one exception to this rule, and that is the pleasure we feel when confronted with beauty. This pleasure Kant calls "disinterested delight [*uninteressiertes Wohlgefallen*]," choosing a different word for it on purpose. We shall later see what an important role this notion plays in that political philosophy that Kant never wrote. He himself alludes to it when, in one of the posthumously published reflections, he writes: "The fact that man is affected by the sheer beauty of nature proves that he is made for and fits into this world [Die schönen Dinge zeigen an, dass der Mensch in die Welt passe und selbst seine Anschauung der Dinge mit den Gesetzen seiner Anschauung stimme]."[63]

Let us suppose for a moment that Kant had written a theodicy, a justification of the Creator before the Tribunal of Reason. We know that he did not; rather, he wrote an essay about the "failure of all philosophical attempts in theodicies," and he proved in the *Critique of Pure Reason* the impossibility of all demonstrations of God's existence (he took Job's position: God's ways are inscrutable). Still, had he written a theodicy, the fact of beauty of things in the world would have played an important part in it—as important as the famous "moral law within me," that is, the fact of human dignity. (Theodicies rely on the argument that, if you look at *the whole,* you will see that the particular, about which you complain, is part and parcel of it and, as such, is justified in its existence. In an early essay [1759] on optimism,[64] Kant took a similar position: "The whole is the best, and everything is good for the sake of the whole." I doubt that he would later have been able to write, as he did there: "I call out to each creature . . . : Hail us, we are! [Heil uns, wir sind!]." But the praise is praise of the "whole," i.e., of the world; in his youth Kant was still willing to pay the price of life for being in the world at all.) This is also the reason why he attacked with such unusual vehemence the "obscurantist sages" who, in "partly nauseous allegories," presented "our world [the earth], the domicile of mankind, completely contemptuously," as

an *inn* . . . where every man putting up there along his journey through life must be prepared to be soon supplanted by a successor; as a *penitentiary* . . . for the chastisement and purification of fallen spirits expelled from heaven . . . ; as a *lunatic asylum* . . . ; as a *cloaca* to which all refuse from other worlds has been conjured . . . [a kind of] privy for the whole universe.[65]

So, let us retain for the moment the following ideas. The world is beautiful and therefore a fit place for men to live in, but individual men would never choose to live again. Man as a moral being is an end in himself, but the human species is subject to progress, which, of course, is somehow in opposition to man as a moral and rational creature, an end in himself.

If I am right that there exists a political philosophy in Kant but that, in contrast to other philosophers, he never wrote it, then it seems obvious that we should be able to find it, if we can find it at all, in his whole work and not just in the few essays that are usually collected under this rubric. If his main works, on the one hand, contain no political implications at all, and if, on the other hand, the peripheral writings dealing with political subjects contain merely peripheral thoughts, unconnected with his strictly philosophical works, then our inquiry would be pointless, at best of antiquarian interest. It would be against the very spirit of Kant to concern ourselves with them, for the passion for erudition remained alien to him. He did not intend, as he noted in his reflections, "to make his head into a piece of parchment to scribble down on it old half-effaced bits of information from archives [Ich werde ja meinen Kopf nicht zu einem Pergament machen, um alte halb-erloschene Nachrichten aus Archiven darauf nachzukritzeln]."[66]

Let us start with something that today will hardly surprise anyone but that still is worth taking into consideration. No one before Kant or after him, except Sartre, wrote a famous philosophical book that he entitled *Critique*. We know both too little and too much why Kant chose this surprising and somewhat derogatory title, as though he meant no more than to criticize all his predecessors. To be sure, he meant more than this with the word, but the negative connotation was never altogether absent from his mind: "The whole philosophy of true reason is directed solely toward this negative benefit"[67]—namely, to make reason "pure," to assure that no experience, no sensation, would introduce itself into reason's thinking. The word may have been suggested to him, as he himself pointed out, by the "age of criticism," i.e., the Age of Enlightenment, and he remarks that it is "that merely negative attitude which constitutes enlightenment proper."[68] Enlightenment means, in this context, liberation from prejudices, from authorities, a purifying event.

Our age is, in especial degree, the age of criticism, and to such criticism everything must submit. Religion . . . and legislation . . . may seek to exempt themselves from it. But they then awaken just suspicion, and cannot claim the sincere respect which reason accords only to that which has been able to sustain the test of free and open examination.[69]

The result of such criticism is *Selbstdenken,* to "use your own mind." Using his own mind, Kant discovered the "scandal of reason," that is, that it is not just tradition and authority that lead us astray but the faculty of reason itself. Hence, "critique" means an attempt to discover reason's "sources and limits." Kant thus believed that his critique was a mere "propaedeutic to the system," and "critique" is here placed in opposition to "doctrine." Kant believed, it seems, that what was wrong with traditional metaphysics was not "doctrine" itself. Thus critique means "to lay down the complete architectonic plan . . . to guarantee . . . the completeness and certainty of the structure in all its parts."[70] As such, it will make it possible to evaluate all other philosophical systems. This, again, is connected with the spirit of the eighteenth century, with its enormous interest in aesthetics, in art and *art criticism,* the goal of which was to lay down rules for taste, to establish standards in the arts.

The word critique, finally and most importantly, stands in a twofold opposition to dogmatic metaphysics on the one hand, to skepticism on the other. The answer to both was: Critical thinking. Succumb to neither. As such, it is a new way of thinking and not a mere preparation for a new doctrine. Hence, it is not as though the seemingly negative business of critique could be followed by the seemingly positive business of system-making. This is what indeed took place, but, from a Kantian viewpoint, this was but another dogmatism. (Kant never was quite clear and unequivocal on this point; could he have seen to what exercises in sheer speculation his *Critique* would liberate Fichte, Schelling, and Hegel, he might have been a bit clearer.) Philosophy itself, according to Kant, has become critical in the age of criticism and Enlightenment—the time when man had come of age.

It would be a great error to believe that critical thinking stands somewhere between dogmatism and skepticism. It is actually the way to leave these alternatives behind. (In biographical terms: it is Kant's way of overcoming both the old metaphysical schools—Wolff and Leibniz—and the new skepticism of Hume, which had roused him from dogmatic slumber.) We all start out as dogmatists in one way or the other; we are either dogmatic in philosophy or we solve all problems by believing in the dogmas of some church, in revelation. One's first reaction against this, triggered off by the inescapable experience of *many* dogmas, all of which claim to possess *the* truth, is skepticism: the conclusion that there is no such a thing as truth, that therefore I may either arbitrarily choose some dogmatic doctrine (arbitrarily with regard to truth: my choice may be prompted simply by various interests and be entirely pragmatic). Or I may simply shrug my shoulders about so profitless a business. The real skeptic, the one who states, "There is no truth," will immediately be answered by the dogmatist: "But you imply, by stating this, that you *do* believe in truth; you claim validity for your statement that there is no truth." It seems that he has won the argument. But no more than the argument. The skeptic can reply, "This is sheer sophistry. You know very well what I mean even though I cannot utter it in words without an apparent contradiction." Whereupon the dogmatist will say, "See? Language itself is against you." And, since the dogmatist is usually a rather aggressive fellow, he will proceed and say, "Since you are intelligent enough to understand the contradiction, I must conclude that you have an *interest* in destroying truth; you are a nihilist." The critical position stands against both of these. It recommends itself by its modesty. It would say: "Perhaps men, though they have a notion, an idea, of truth for regulating their mental processes, are not capable, as finite beings, of *the* truth. (The Socratic: 'No man is wise.') Meanwhile, they are quite able to inquire into such human faculties as they have been given—we do not know by whom or how, but we have to live with them. Let us analyze what we can know *and* what we cannot." This is why his book is entitled the *Critique* of pure reason.

Sixth Session

WE WERE DISCUSSING the term "critique," which Kant, according to his own understanding, had taken from the Age of Enlightenment; and if we went beyond Kant's self-interpretation in our presentation, we still remained within Kant's spirit. As he himself said, posterity often "understands an author better than he understood himself."[71] We said that Kant, though the negative spirit of criticism was never absent from his mind, meant, by critique, not a criticism of "books and systems but of the faculty of reason as such";[72] we also said that he believed that he had found the way out of the sterile choice between dogmatism and skepticism, which usually is resolved in "complete indifferentism—the mother, in all sciences, of chaos and night."[73] I told you, in the dialogue between the skeptic and the dogmatist, of the skeptic who exclaims, when confronted with so many truths (or rather with people, each of whom pretends to have *the* truth, and with the fierce battle between them), "There is no truth" and therewith speaks the charmed words that unite all dogmatists. Into this battle the critic enters and interrupts the shouting match: "Both of you, dogmatists and skeptics, seem to have the same concept of truth, namely, something which by definition excludes all other truths, so that all of them become mutually exclusive. Perhaps," he says, "there is something wrong with your concept of truth. Perhaps," he adds, "men, finite beings, have a notion of truth but cannot have, possess, the truth. Let us first analyze this faculty of ours which tells us that there is truth." No doubt, the "Critique limits speculative reason, it is indeed *negative*"; but to deny that, for this reason, "the service which the Critique renders is *positive* in character would be like saying that the police are of no positive benefit, inasmuch as their main business is merely to prevent the violence of which citizens stand in mutual fear, in order that each may pursue his vocation in peace and security."[74] When Kant was through with his Critique, the analysis of our cognitive faculties, Mendelssohn called him the *Alles-Zermalmer,* the "all-destroyer," namely, the destroyer of any belief that I can *know* in so-called metaphysical matters and that there can be such a "science" as metaphysics, having the same validity as other sciences.

But Kant himself did not see the clearly destructive side of his enterprise. He did not understand that he had actually *dismantled* the whole machinery that had lasted, though often under attack, for many centuries, deep into the modern age. He thought, quite in tune with the spirit of the time, that the "loss affects only the monopoly of the Schools, but by no means the interest of men," who will finally be rid of the "subtle but ineffectual distinctions" that in any case have never "succeeded in reaching the public mind [*das Publikum*] or in exercising the slightest influence on its convictions."[75] (I am reading to you from the two prefaces to the *Critique of Pure Reason,* which are addressed to what Kant calls elsewhere "the reading public.")

And the polemical point is again against "the arrogant pretensions of the Schools," which claim to be the sole "possessors of truths," truths that are not only "matters of general human concern" but also "within the reach of the great mass of men—ever to be held in the highest esteem by us."[76] So much for the universities. As far as governments are concerned, Kant adds that, should they think it proper to interfere, it would be much wiser "to support such critique . . . than to support the ridiculous despotism of the Schools, which raise a loud cry of public danger when somebody destoys their cobwebs, to which the public has never paid any attention and the loss of which it therefore can never feel."[77]

I have read to you more than I originally intended, partly to give you an inkling of the atmosphere in which these books were written, and partly because the consequences—though they did not result in an armed uprising—were, after all, a bit more serious than Kant himself foresaw. As for the atmosphere: the mentality of the Enlightenment, on the highest level, did not last for long, and it may best be illustrated by contrasting it with the attitude of the next generation, well represented by the young Hegel:

> Philosophy by its very nature is something esoteric which is not made for the mob nor is it capable of being prepared for the mob; philosophy is philosophy only to the extent that it is the very opposite of the intellect and even more the opposite of common sense, by which we understand the local and temporary limitations of generations; in its relation to this common sense, the world of philosophy as such is a world turned upside down.[78]

For

> the beginning of philosophy must be a lifting oneself up above that kind of truth given by common consciousness, the premonition of a higher truth.[79]

If we are thinking in terms of progress, this certainly is a "relapse" into what philosophy had been since its beginning, and Hegel repeats the story Plato told about Thales, with a great show of indignation at the laughing Thracian peasant girl. Kant is not free of responsibility for the fact that his critical philosophy was almost immediately understood as another "system" and was then attacked as such by the next generation, when the spirit of the Enlightenment, which had inspired it, was lost.

Still, when this "relapse" had run its course with the systems of German idealism, the generation of Kant's sons, the generation of what could have been his grandsons and great-grandsons—from Marx to Nietzsche—decided, seemingly under the influence of Hegel, to leave philosophy altogether. If you think in terms of the history of ideas, you could say that the consequences of the Critique of Reason could have been either the establishment of critical thinking or the "insight" that reason and philosophical thinking are good for nothing and that "critique" means the destruction, in thought, of whatever it seizes upon, as against Kant's notion of "critique" as limitation and purification.

There exists another book that uses the word critique in its title, and one I had forgotten to mention. Marx's *Capital* was originally called *The Critique of Political Economy*, and Marx's Preface to its second edition mentions the dialectical method as being at the same time "critical and revolutionary." Marx knew what he was doing. He had called Kant, as many did after him and as Hegel had done before him, "the philosopher of the French Revolution." For Marx, but not for Kant, what joined theory to practice was critique; it related them and, as the saying goes, mediated between them. It was the example of the French Revolution, an event that had been preceded by the Age of Criticism and Enlightenment, that suggested that the *theoretical* dismantling of the *ancien régime* had been followed by the *practice* of destroying it. This, the example seemed to say, is how "the idea seizes the masses." The point here is not whether this is true—whether this is the way revolutions come about; the point is rather that Marx thought in these terms because he saw Kant's huge enterprise as the greatest work of the Enlightenment and believed with Kant that enlightenment and revolution belong together. (For Kant "the middle term" that links and provides a transition from theory to practice is judgment; he had in mind the practitioner—for example, the doctor or lawyer, who first learns theory and then practices medicine or law, and whose practice consists in applying the rules he has learned to particular cases.)[80]

To think critically, to blaze the trail of thought through prejudices, through unexamined opinions and beliefs, is an old concern of philosophy, which we may date, insofar as it is a conscious enterprise, to the Socratic midwifery in Athens. Kant was not unaware of this connection. He said explicitly that he wished to proceed "in Socratic fashion" and to silence all objectors "by the clearest proof of [their] ignorance."[81] Unlike Socrates, he believed in a "future system of metaphysics,"[82] but what he finally bequeathed to posterity were critiques and no system. Socrates' method consisted in emptying his partners of all unfounded beliefs and "windeggs"—the mere phantasies that filled their minds.[83] According to Plato, he did this by the art of *krinein*, of sorting out and separating and distinguishing (*technē diakritikē*, the art of discrimination).[84] According to Plato (but not according to Socrates), the result is "the purification of the soul from conceits that stand in the way of knowledge"; according to Socrates, no knowledge follows the examination, and none of his partners was ever delivered of a child that was no windegg. Socrates taught nothing; he never knew the answers to the questions he asked. He did the examining for examining's sake, not for the sake of knowledge. Had he known what courage, justice, piety, etc., were, he would no longer have had the urge to examine them, i.e., to think about them. Socrates' uniqueness lies in this concentration on thinking itself, regardless of results. There is no ulterior motive or ulterior purpose for the whole enterprise. An unexamined life is not worth living. That is all there is to it. What he actually did was to make *public*, in discourse, the thinking process—that dialogue that soundlessly goes on within me, between me and myself; he *performed* in the marketplace the way the flute-player performed at a banquet. It is sheer performance, sheer activity. And just as the flute-player has to follow certain rules in order to perform well, Socrates discovered the only rule that holds sway over thinking—the rule of consistency (as Kant was to call it in the *Critique of Judgment*)[85] or, as it was later called, the axiom of noncontradiction. This axiom, which for Socrates was "logical" (Do not talk or think non-sense) as well as "ethical" (It is better to be at odds with multitudes than, *being one*, to be at odds with yourself, namely, to contradict yourself),[86] became with Aristotle the first principle of thinking, but of thinking only. However, with Kant, whose whole moral teaching actually rests on it, it became again part of ethics; because ethics in Kant is also based on a thought process: Act so that the maxim of your action can be willed by you to become a general law, that is, a law to which you yourself would be subject. It is, again, the same general rule—Do not contradict yourself (not your self but your thinking ego)—that determines both thinking and acting.

The Socratic fashion was of importance to Kant for another reason. Socrates was a member of no sect, and he founded no school. He became the figure of *the* philosopher because he took on all comers in the marketplace—was entirely unprotected, open to all questioners, to all demands to give an account of and to live up to what he said. The schools and sects are unenlightened (in Kantian parlance) because they depend on the doctrines of their founders. Ever since Plato's Academy, they have stood in opposition to "public opinion," to society at large, to the "they"; but that does not mean that they rely on no authority. The model is always the school of the Pythagoreans, whose conflicts could be solved by appeal to the authority of the founder: to the *autos epha,* the *ipse dixit,* the "he himself said so." In other words, the unthinking dogmatism of the many is countered by the select but equally unthinking dogmatism of the few.

If we now consider once more the relation of philosophy to politics, it is clear that the art of critical thinking always has political implications. And it had the gravest consequences in the case of Socrates. Unlike dogmatic thought, which indeed may spread new and "dangerous" beliefs but does so behind the protective walls of a school that takes care of the *arcana,* the secret, esoteric doctrine, and, again, unlike speculative thought, which rarely bothers anyone, critical thought is in principle anti-authoritarian. And, as far as the authorities are concerned, the worst thing is that you cannot catch it, cannot seize it. The accusation in the trial of Socrates—that he introduced new gods into the polis—was a trumped-up charge; Socrates taught nothing, least of all new gods. But the other charge, that he corrupted the young, was not without grounds. The trouble with men of critical thought is that they "make the pillars of the best-known truths shake wherever they let their eyes fall" (Lessing). This certainly was Kant's case. Kant was the all-destroyer though he never entered the marketplace and though the *Critique of Pure Reason,* one of the most difficult, though certainly not obscure, books in philosophy, is not likely ever to become popular, even among Kant's beloved "reading public." The point, however, is that Kant, in distinction from almost all other philosophers, regretted this deeply and never gave up hope that it would be possible to popularize his thought, that the "narrow footpath for the few would become a high-road [for all]."[87] In a curiously apologetic tone, he writes to Mendelssohn on August 16, 1783, two years after publication of the *Critique of Pure Reason:*

> [Though the *Critique* is] the outcome of reflections which had occupied me for a period of at least twelve years, I brought it

to completion in the greatest haste within some four or five months . . . with little thought of . . . rendering it easy of comprehension by the reader, . . . since otherwise, had I . . . sought to give it a more popular form, the work would probably never have been completed at all. This *defect* can, however, be gradually removed, now that the work exists in a rough form.[88]

Critical thinking, according to Kant and according to Socrates, exposes itself to "the test of free and open examination," and this means that the more people participate in it, the better. Hence, in 1781, immediately after publication of the *Critique of Pure Reason,* Kant "devised a plan for popularizing" it. "For," he wrote in 1783, "every philosophical work must be susceptible of popularity; if not, it probably conceals nonsense beneath a fog of seeming sophistication."[89] What Kant hoped for in his hope for popularization—so strange in a philosopher, a tribe that usually has such strong sectarian tendencies—was that the circle of his examiners would gradually be enlarged. The Age of Enlightenment is the age of "the public use of one's reason"; hence, the most important political freedom for Kant was not, as for Spinoza, the *libertas philosophandi* but the freedom to speak and to publish.

The word "freedom" has many meanings in Kant, as we shall see; but political freedom is defined quite unequivocally and consistently throughout his work as *"to make public use of one's reason at every point."*[90] And, "by the public use of one's reason I understand the use which a person makes of it as a scholar before the reading public." There are restrictions on this use, indicated by the words "as a scholar"; the scholar is not the same as the citizen; he is a member of a very different kind of community, namely, "a society of world citizens," and it is in this capacity that he addresses the public. (Kant's example is quite clear: an officer in service has no right to refuse to obey. "But the right to make remarks on errors in the military service and to lay them before the public for judgment cannot equitably be refused him as a scholar," that is, as a world citizen.)[91]

Freedom of speech and thought, as we understand it, is the right of an individual to express himself and his opinion in order to be able to persuade others to share his viewpoint. This presupposes that I am capable of making up my mind all by myself and that the claim I have on the government is to permit me to propagandize whatever I have already fixed in my mind. Kant's view of this matter is very different. He believes that the very faculty of thinking depends on its public use; without "the test of free and open examination," no thinking and no opinion-formation are possible. Reason is not made "to isolate itself but to get into community with others."[92] Kant's position on this matter is quite noteworthy because it is not the position of the political man but of the philosopher or thinker. Thinking, as Kant agreed with Plato, is the silent dialogue of myself with myself (*das Reden mit sich selbst*), and that thinking is a "solitary business" (as Hegel once remarked) is one of the few things on which all thinkers were agreed. Also, it is of course by no means true that you need or can even bear the company of others when you happen to be busy thinking; yet, unless you can somehow communicate and expose to the test of others, either orally or in writing, whatever you may have found out when you were alone, this faculty exerted in solitude will disappear. In the words of Jaspers, truth is what I can communicate. Truth in the sciences is dependent on the experiment that can be repeated by others; it requires general validity. Philosophic truth has no such general validity. What it must have, what Kant demanded in the *Critique of Judgment* of judgments of taste, is "general communicability." "For it is a natural vocation of mankind to communicate and speak one's mind, especially in all matters concerning man as such."[93]

Seventh Session

WE WERE TALKING about the political implications of critical thinking and the notion that critical thinking implies communicability. Now communicability obviously implies a community of men who can be addressed and who are listening and can be listened to. To the question, Why are there men rather than Man? Kant would have answered: In order that they may talk to one another. For men in the plural, and hence for mankind—for the species, as it were, that we belong to—"it is a natural vocation . . . to communicate and speak one's mind"—a remark I have quoted before. Kant is aware that he disagrees with most thinkers in asserting that thinking, though a solitary business, depends on others to be possible at all:

> It is said: the freedom to speak or to write can be taken away from us by the powers-that-be, but the freedom to think can-

not be taken from us through them at all. However, how much and how correctly would we think if we did not think in community with others to whom we communicate our thoughts and who communicate theirs to us! Hence, we may safely state that the external power which deprives man of the freedom to communicate his thoughts *publicly* also takes away his freedom to *think,* the only treasure left to us in our civic life and through which alone there may be a remedy against all evils of the present state of affairs.[94]

We can look at this factor of publicity, necessary for critical thinking, from still another viewpoint. What Socrates actually did when he brought philosophy from the heavens down to earth and began to examine opinions about what went on between men was that he extracted from every statement its hidden or latent implications; that is what his midwifery actually amounted to. As the midwife helps the child to come to light to be inspected, so Socrates brings to light the implications to be inspected. (That is what Kant did when he complained about progress: he extracted the implications of this concept; that is what we did here when we protested against the organic metaphor.) Critical thinking to a very large extent consists of this kind of "analysis." This examination, in turn, presupposes that everyone is willing and able to render an account of what he thinks and says. Plato, having gone through the school of Socratic midwifery, was the first to write philosophy in the way we still recognize as philosophy and what later, with Aristotle, became the treatise. He saw the difference between himself and the "wise men" of old, the Presocratics, in the fact that they, wise though they were, never gave an account of their thoughts. There they were, with their great insights; but when you asked them a question, they remained silent. *Logon didonai,* "to give an account"—not to prove, but to be able to say how one came to an opinion and for what reasons one formed it—is actually what separates Plato from all of his predecessors. The term itself is political in origin: to render accounts is what Athenian citizens asked of their politicians, not only in money matters but in matters of politics. They could be held responsible. And this—holding oneself and everyone else responsible and answerable for what he thought and taught—was what transformed into philosophy that search for knowledge and for truth that had sprung up in Ionia. This transformation had already come about with the Sophists, who have rightly been called the

representatives of Enlightenment in Greece; it was then
sharpened into a method of question and answer by Socrates'
midwifery. This is the origin of critical thought, whose greatest
representative in the modern age, perhaps in all postclassical
ages, was Kant, who was entirely conscious of its implications. In
one of his most important reflections, he writes as follows:

> *Quaestio facti,* the question of fact, is in which way one has first
> obtained a concept; *quaestio juris,* the juridical question, is with
> what right one possesses this concept and uses it.[95]

To think critically applies not only to doctrines and concepts one
receives from others, to the prejudices and traditions one inher-
its; it is precisely by applying critical standards to one's own
thought that one learns the art of critical thought.

And this application one cannot learn without publicity, without the testing that arises from contact with other people's thinking.
In order to show how it works, I shall read to you two personal passages from letters Kant wrote in the 1770s to Marcus
Herz:

> You know that I do not approach reasonable objections with
> the intention merely of refuting them, but that in thinking
> them over I always weave them into my judgments, and af-
> ford them the opportunity of overturning all my most
> cherished beliefs. I entertain the hope that by thus viewing
> my judgments impartially from the standpoint of others some
> third view that will improve upon my previous insight may be
> obtainable.[96]

You see that *impartiality* is obtained by taking the viewpoints of
others into account; impartiality is not the result of some higher
standpoint that would then actually settle the dispute by being
altogether above the melée. In the second letter, Kant makes this
even clearer:

> [The mind needs a reasonable amount of relaxations and
> diversions to maintain its mobility] that it may be enabled to
> view the object afresh from every side, and so to enlarge its
> point of view from a microscopic to a general outlook that it
> adopts in turn every conceivable standpoint, verifying the ob-
> servations of each by means of all the others.[97]

Here the word "impartiality" is not mentioned. In its stead, we
find the notion that one can "enlarge" one's own thought so as to
take into account the thoughts of others. The "enlargement of

the mind" plays a crucial role in the *Critique of Judgment*. It is accomplished by "comparing our judgment with the possible rather than the actual judgments of others, and by putting ourselves in the place of any other man."[98] The faculty that makes this possible is called imagination. When you read the paragraphs in the *Critique of Judgment* and compare them with the letters just quoted, you will see that the former contain no more than the conceptualization of these very personal remarks. Critical thinking is possible only where the standpoints of all others are open to inspection. Hence, critical thinking, while still a solitary business, does not cut itself off from "all others." To be sure, it still goes on in isolation, but by the force of imagination it makes the others present and thus moves in a space that is potentially public, open to all sides; in other words, it adopts the position of Kant's world citizen. To think with an enlarged mentality means that one trains one's imagination to go visiting. (Compare the right to visit in *Perpetual Peace*.)

I must warn you here of a very common and easy misunderstanding. The trick of critical thinking does not consist in an enormously enlarged empathy through which one can know what actually goes on in the mind of all others. To think, according to Kant's understanding of enlightenment, means *Selbstdenken,* to think for oneself, "which is the maxim of a never-passive reason. To be given to such passivity is called prejudice,"[99] and enlightenment is, first of all, liberation from prejudice. To accept what goes on in the minds of those whose "standpoint" (actually, the place where they stand, the conditions they are subject to, which always differ from one individual to the next, from one class or group as compared to another) is not my own would mean no more than passively to accept their thought, that is, to exchange their prejudices for the prejudices proper to my own station. "Enlarged thought" is the result of first "abstracting from the limitations which contingently attach to our own judgment," of disregarding its "subjective private conditions..., by which so many are limited," that is, disregarding what we usually call self-interest, which, according to Kant, is not enlightened or capable of enlightenment but is in fact limiting. The greater the reach—the larger the realm in which the enlightened individual is able to move from standpoint to standpoint—the more "general" will be his thinking. This generality, however, is not the generality of the concept— for example, the concept "house," under which one can then subsume various kinds of individual buildings. It is, on the contrary, closely connected with particulars, with the particular conditions of the standpoints one has to go through in order to arrive at one's own "general standpoint." This general standpoint we spoke of earlier as impartiality; it is a viewpoint from which to look upon, to watch, to form judgments, or, as Kant himself says, to reflect upon human affairs. It does not tell one how *to act*. It does not even tell one how to apply the wisdom, found by virtue of occupying a "general standpoint," to the particulars of political life. (Kant had no experience of such action whatsoever and could have had none in the Prussia of Frederick II.) Kant does tell one how to take others into account; he does not tell one how to combine with them in order to act.

Which brings us to this question: Is the general standpoint merely the standpoint of the spectator? (How serious Kant was about the enlargement of his own mentality is indicated by the fact that he introduced and taught a course in physical geography at the university. He was also an eager reader of all sorts of travel reports, and he—who never left Königsberg—knew his way around in both London and Italy; he said he had no time to travel precisely because he wanted to know so much about so many countries.) In Kant's own mind it was certainly the standpoint of the world citizen. But does this easy phrase of idealists, "citizen of the world," make sense? To be a citizen means among other things to have responsibilities, obligations, and rights, all of which make sense only if they are territorially limited. Kant's world citizen was actually a *Weltbetrachter,* a world-spectator. Kant knew quite well that a world government would be the worst tyranny imaginable.

In Kant himself, in his last years, this perplexity comes to the fore in the seeming contradiction between his almost boundless admiration for the French Revolution and his equally boundless opposition to any revolutionary undertaking on the part of the French citizens. The passages I shall read to you were all written at about the same time. But before we proceed, let me remind you that Marx called Kant the philosopher of the French Revolution, as Heine had earlier. More important, perhaps, this evaluation had a solid foundation in the self-understanding of the Revolution itself. Sieyès, famous author of the *Tiers Etat* and one of the founders of the Jacobin Club, who then became one of the most important members of the Constituent Assembly, the assembly commissioned to draft the French Constitution,

seems to have known Kant and to have been influenced to some
degree by his philosophy. At any rate, a friend of his, Theremin,
approached Kant to say that Sieyès intended to introduce Kant's
philosophy in France because "l'étude de cette philosophie par
les Français serait un complément de la Révolution [the study of
this philosophy by Frenchmen would complement the Revolu-
tion]."[100] Kant's answer is lost.

Kant's reaction to the French Revolution, at first and even
second glance, is by no means unequivocal. To anticipate: he never
wavered in his estimation of the grandeur of what he called the
"recent event," and he hardly ever wavered in his condemnation
of all those who had prepared it. I shall start with the most
famous of his utterances in this connection; moreover, it contains,
in a sense, the key to the seeming contradiction in his attitude.

This event [the Revolution] consists neither in momentous
deeds nor misdeeds committed by men whereby what was
great among men is made small or what was small is made
great, nor in ancient splendid political structures which van-
ish as if by magic while others come forth in their place as if
from the depths of the earth. No, nothing of the sort. It is
simply the mode of thinking of the spectators which reveals
itself publicly in this game of great transformations, and
manifests such a general yet disinterested sympathy for the
players on one side against those on the other, even at the risk
that this partiality could become very disadvantageous for
them if discovered. Owing to its generality, this mode of
thinking demonstrates a character of the human race at large
and all at once; owing to its disinterestedness, a moral
character of humanity, at least in its predisposition, a character which not only permits people to hope for progress toward the better, but is already itself progress insofar as its
capacity is sufficient for the present.

The revolution of a gifted people which we have seen unfolding in our day may succeed or miscarry; it may be filled
with misery and atrocities to the point that a sensible man,
were he boldly to hope to execute it successfully the second
time, would never resolve to make the experiment at such
cost—this revolution, I say, nonetheless finds in the hearts of
all spectators (who are not engaged in this game themselves) a
wishful participation that borders closely on enthusiasm, the
very expression of which is fraught with danger; this sympathy, therefore, can have no other cause than a moral predisposition in the human race.

. . . Monetary rewards could not elevate the adversaries of

the revolution to the zeal and grandeur of soul which the
pure concept of right produced in [the revolutionaries]; and
even the concept of honor among the old martial nobility (an
analogue to enthusiasm) vanished before the weapons of
those who kept in view the right of the people to which they
belonged and of which they considered themselves the guar-
dians; with what exaltation the uninvolved public looking on
sympathized then without the least intention of assisting. . . .

Now I claim to be able to predict to the human race—even
without prophetic insight—according to the aspects and
omens of our day, the attainment of this goal. That is, I predict its progress toward the better which, from now on, turns
out to be no longer completely reversible. For such a
phenomenon in human history *is not to be forgotten*. . . .

But even if the end viewed in connection with this event
should not now be attained, even if the revolution or reform
of a national constitution should finally miscarry, or, after
some time had elapsed, everything should relapse into its
former rut (as politicians now predict), that philosophical
prophecy still would lose nothing of its force. For that event is
too important, too much interwoven with the interest of humanity, and its influence too widely propagated in all areas of
the world to not be recalled on any favorable occasion by the
peoples which would then be roused to a repetition of new
efforts of this kind. . . . To him who does not consider what
happens in just one people but also has regard to the whole
scope of all the peoples on earth who will gradually come to
participate in these events, this reveals the prospect of an
immeasurable time.[101]

Eighth Session

IN WHAT I READ TO YOU from *The Contest of the Faculties* (Part II,
sections 6 and 7), Kant said explicitly that he was not concerned
with the deeds and misdeeds of men that make empires rise and
fall, make small what was formerly great and great what was
formerly small. The importance of the occurrence (*Begebenheit*)
is for him exclusively in the eye of the beholder, in the opinion
of the onlookers who proclaim their attitude in public. Their
reaction to the event proves the "moral character" of mankind.
Without this sympathetic participation, the "meaning" of the
occurrence would be altogether different or simply nonexistent.
For it is this sympathy that inspires hope,

the hope that, after many revolutions, with all their trans-
forming effects, the highest purpose of nature, a *cosmopolitan
existence,* will at last be realized within which all the original
capacities of the human race may be developed.[102]

From this, however, one should not conclude that Kant sided
in the least with the men of future revolutions. In a footnote to
the passage from *The Contest of the Faculties,* he makes this very
explicit: there are "rights of the people" that no ruler dares to
contest publicly for fear that the people will rise up against him;
and this they would do for the sake of freedom alone, even if
they were well fed, powerfully protected, and had "no lack of
welfare to complain of." The rights of men, implying the right of
the people to be "colegislators," are sacred. And yet:

> These rights . . . always remain an idea which can be fulfilled
> only on condition that the *means* employed to do so are com-
> patible with morality. This limiting condition must not be
> overstepped by the people, who may not therefore pursue
> their rights by revolution, which is at all times unjust.[103]

If we had no more than this footnote, we might suspect that
Kant was cautious when he appended it; but the same warning is
repeated in a number of other passages. We turn to *Perpetual
Peace,* where his position is best explained:

> If a violent revolution, engendered by a bad constitution, in-
> troduces by illegal means a more legal constitution, to lead the
> people back to the earlier constitution would not be permit-
> ted; but, while the revolution lasted, each person who openly
> or covertly shared in it would have justly incurred the
> punishment due to those who rebel.[104]

For, as he writes in the same vein in *The Metaphysics of Morals,*

> if a revolution has succeeded and a new constitution has been
> established, the unlawfulness of its origin and success cannot
> free the subjects from the obligation to accommodate them-
> selves as good citizens to the new order of things.[105]

Hence, whatever the status quo may be, good or bad, rebellion is
never legitimate. To be sure, if

> The rights of the people are injured, [then] no injustice be-
> falls the tyrant when he is deposed. There can be no doubt on
> this point. Nevertheless, it is in the highest degree illegitimate
> for the subjects to seek their rights in this way. If they fail in

the struggle and are then subjected to severe punishment, they cannot complain about injustice any more than the tyrant could if they had succeeded.[106]

What you see here clearly is the clash between the principle according to which you should act and the principle according to which you judge. For Kant condemns the very action whose results he then affirms with a satisfaction bordering on enthusiasm. This clash is not a mere matter of theory; in 1798, Kant was once more confronted with a rebellion, one of the many rebellions of Ireland against the then "legitimate" authority of England. According to an acquaintance, as recorded in the diary of Abegg, he believed the rebellion to be legitimate and even expressed hope for a future republic of England.[107] Again, it was a mere matter of opinion, the judgment of the spectator. And he writes in the same vein:

> I cannot admit the expression used even by intelligent men: A certain people (engaged in elaborating civil freedom) is not yet ripe for freedom; the bondmen of a landed proprietor are not yet ripe for freedom; and thus also, men in general are not yet ripe for freedom of belief. According to such a presupposition freedom will never arrive; for we cannot *ripen* to this freedom unless we are already set free—we must be free in order to be able to use our faculties purposively in freedom [and] we never ripen for reason except through our *own* efforts, which we can make only when we are free.... [To maintain that people who are subject to bonds] are essentially unfit for freedom ... is to usurp the prerogatives of Divinity itself, which created man for freedom.[108]

The reason why you should not engage in what, if successful, you would applaud is the "transcendental principle of publicness," which rules all political action. Kant sets forth this principle in *Perpetual Peace* (Appendix II), where he calls the conflict between the engaged actor and the judging spectator a "conflict of politics with morality." The overriding principle is:

> All actions relating to the right of other men are unjust if their maxim is not consistent with publicity ... [for a] maxim which I cannot divulge publicly without defeating my own purpose must be kept secret if it is to succeed; and, if I cannot publicly avow it without inevitably exciting general opposition to my project, the ... opposition which can be foreseen a priori is due only to the injustice with which the maxim threatens everyone.[109]

Just as the wrongness of despotism can be demonstrated, because "no ruler ever dared to say openly that he does not recognize any rights of the people against himself," so the wrongness of rebellion "is apparent from the fact that, if the maxim upon which [the people] would act were *publicly acknowledged*, it would defeat its own purpose. This maxim would therefore have to be kept secret."[110] The maxim of "political expediency," for instance, would "necessarily defeat its own purpose if made public"; on the other hand, a people engaged in the establishment of a new government could not "publish its intention to revolt" because "no state would be possible" on this condition, and to establish a state "was the purpose of the people."

The two main arguments against this reasoning are mentioned by Kant himself. First, the principle is "only negative, i.e., it only serves for the recognition of what is not just, [and] we cannot infer conversely that the maxims which bear publicity are therefore just."[111] In other words, opinion too, especially if it is not the disinterested opinion of the onlooker but the partial, uncritical opinion of interested citizens, may be wrong. Second, the analogy between ruler and ruled is wrong: "no one who has decidedly superior power needs to conceal his plans." He therefore proposes an "affirmative and transcendental principle":

All maxims which *stand in need* of publicity in order not to fail their end agree with politics and right combined.[112]

This solution of "the conflict of politics with morality" is derived from Kant's moral philosophy, in which man as a single individual, consulting nothing but his own reason, finds the maxim that is not self-contradictory, from which he can then derive an Imperative. Publicness is already the criterion of rightness in his moral philosophy. Thus, for instance, "Everybody considers the moral law as something he can declare publicly, but he considers his maxims as something which must be hidden" ("Jeder sieht das moralische Gesetz als ein solches an, welches er *offentlich* deklarieren kann, aber jeder sieht seine Maximen als solche an, die verborgen werden müssen").[113] Private maxims must be subjected to an examination by which I find out whether I can declare them publicly. Morality here is the coincidence of the private and the public. To insist on the privacy of the maxim is to be evil. To be evil, therefore, is characterized by withdrawal from the public realm. Morality means being fit to be *seen,* and this not only by men but, in the last instance, by God, the omniscient knower of the heart (*der Herzenskundige*).

Man, insofar as he does anything at all, lays down the law; he is the legislator. But one can be this legislator only if one is oneself free; whether the same maxim is valid for the bondsman as for the free man is open to question. And even if you accept Kant's solution as stated here, the precondition obviously is the "freedom of the pen," that is, the existence of a public space for opinion, at least, if not for action. For Kant, the moment to rebel is the moment when freedom of opinion is abolished. Not to rebel then is to be unable to answer the old Machiavellian argument against morality: If you do not resist evil, the evildoers will do as they please. Though it is true that, by resisting evil, you are likely to be involved in evil, your care for the world takes precedence in politics over your care for your self—whether this self is your body or your soul. (Machiavelli's "I love my native city more than my soul" is only a variation of: I love the world and its future more than my life or my self.)

Actually, there are two assumptions in Kant that permit him to extract himself thus easily from the conflict. He is aware of one of them in his polemics with Moses Mendelssohn, who had denied Lessing's "progress of mankind as a whole": Mendelssohn said, as quoted by Kant:

> "Man as an individual progresses; but mankind constantly fluctuates between fixed limits. Regarded as a whole, mankind maintains roughly the same level of morality, the same degree of religion and irreligion, of virtue and vice, of happiness and misery."[114]

Kant replies that, without the assumption of progress, nothing would make sense; progress may be interrupted, but it is never broken off. He appeals to an "inborn duty," the same argument that he uses in the *Critique of Practical Reason*: an inborn voice says: Thou shalt, and it would be a contradiction to assume that I cannot where my own reason tells me that I should (*ultra posse nemo obligatur:* what exceeds the possible obliges no one).[115] The duty appealed to in this case is that "of influencing posterity in such a way that it will make constant progress" (hence progress must be possible), and Kant asserts that, without this assumption, "the hope for better times to come," no action is possible at all; for this hope alone has inspired "right-thinking men" to "do something for the common good."[116] Well, we know today that we can *date* the idea of progress, and we know that men have always acted, i.e., long before this idea appeared.

The second and even more important assumption held by Kant concerns the nature of evil. Machiavelli assumes that evil will spread wildly if men do not resist it even at the risk of doing evil themselves. Kant, on the contrary, and somehow in agreement with the tradition, believes that evil by its very nature is self-destructive. Hence:

> The end of *man* as an entire species ... will be brought by providence [sometimes he says "nature"] to a successful issue, even though the ends of *men* as individuals run in a diametrically opposite direction. For the very conflict of individual inclinations, which is the source of all evil, gives reason a free hand to master them all; it thus gives predominance not to evil, which destroys itself, but to good, which continues to maintain itself once it has been established.[117]

And here again the perspective of the onlooker is decisive. Look at history as a whole. What kind of a spectacle would that be without the assumption of progress? The alternatives for Kant are either regress, which would produce despair, or eternal sameness, which would bore us to death. I quote the following passage to underline once more the importance of the onlooker:

> It is a sight fit for a god to watch a virtuous man grappling with adversity and evil temptations and yet managing to hold out against them. But it is a sight quite unfit ... even for the most ordinary but honest man to see the human race advancing over a period of time towards virtue, and then quickly relapsing the whole way back into vice and misery. It may perhaps be moving and instructive to watch such a drama for a while; but the curtain must eventually descend. For in the long run, it becomes a farce. And even if the actors do not tire of it—for they are fools [Are all actors fools?]—the spectator does, for any single act will be enough for him if he can reasonably conclude from it that the never-ending play will be of eternal sameness [*Einerlei*].[118]

Ninth Session

THE ULTIMATE GUARANTEE that all is well, at least for the spectator, is, as you know from *Perpetual Peace,* nature herself, which can also be called providence or destiny. Nature's "aim is to produce a harmony among men, against their will and indeed through their discord."[119] Discord, indeed, is so important a factor in nature's design that without it no progress can be imagined, and no final harmony could be produced without progress.

The spectator, because he is not involved, can perceive this design of providence or nature, which is hidden from the actor. So we have the spectacle and the spectator on one side, the actors and all the single events and contingent, haphazard happenings on the other. In the context of the French Revolution, it seemed to Kant that the spectator's view carried the ultimate meaning of the event, although this view yielded no maxim for acting. We shall now examine a situation where the opposite somehow seems to be true for Kant: a situation where the single events offer a spectacle that is "sublime," and so do the actors, and where, moreover, the sublimity may well coincide with the hidden design of nature; and still reason, which yields our maxims of action, categorically forbids us to engage in this "sublime" act. We are now dealing with Kant's position on the question of war; and while his sympathies in the matter of revolution were clearly with revolution, his sympathies in the matter of war are clearly and absolutely with peace.

We read in *Perpetual Peace* that "reason, from its throne of supreme moral legislating authority, absolutely condemns war as a legal recourse and makes a state of peace a direct duty, even though peace cannot be established or secured except by a compact among nations."[120] There is not the slightest doubt what our maxim for action should be in this matter. However, this is by no means what the pure onlooker—who does not act and relies entirely on what he sees—would conclude, and the ironical title of the pamphlet more than hints at the possible contradiction. For the original title, *Zum ewigen Frieden,* the satirical inscription of a Dutch innkeeper, means, of course, the cemetery. *That* is the place of Eternal Peace, and the innkeeper offers the beverages that will bring you to this much-longed-for state even in this life. How about peace? Is peace the stagnation that could also be called death? Kant more than once stated his *opinion* on war, formed as the result of his *reflections* on history and the course of mankind, and nowhere does he do so more emphatically than in the *Critique of Judgment,* where he discusses the topic, characteristically enough, in the section on the Sublime:

[W]hat is that which is, even to the savage, an object of the greatest admiration? It is a man who shrinks from nothing, who fears nothing, and therefore does not yield to danger.... Even in the most highly civilized state this peculiar veneration for the soldier remains ... because even [here] it is recognized that his mind is unsubdued by danger. Hence ... in the comparison of a statesman and a general, the aesthetical judgment decides for the latter. War itself ... has something sublime in it.... On the other hand, a long peace generally brings about a predominant commercial spirit and, along with it, low selfishness, cowardice, and effeminacy, and debases the disposition of the people.[121]

This is the judgment of the spectator (i.e., it is aesthetical). What does not enter into the account of the onlooker, who sees the sublime side of war—which is man's courage—is something Kant mentions in a different context in a joke: nations engaged in a war are like two drunkards bludgeoning each other in a china shop.[122] The world (the china shop) is left out of account. But this consideration is taken care of in a way when Kant raises this question: What are wars good for with respect to "progress" and civilization? And here, again, Kant's answer is by no means unequivocal. To be sure, nature's "final design" is a "*cosmopolitan whole*, i.e., a system of all states that are in danger of acting injuriously upon one another." Yet, not only can war, "an unintended enterprise ... stirred up by men's unbridled passions," actually serve, because of its very meaninglessness, as a preparation for the eventual cosmopolitan peace (eventually sheer exhaustion will impose what neither reason nor good will have been able to achieve), but

> In spite of the dreadful afflictions with which it visits the human race, and the perhaps greater afflictions with which the constant preparation for it in time of peace oppresses them, yet is it ... a motive for developing all talents serviceable for culture to the highest possible pitch.[123]

In short, war "is not so incurably bad as the deadness of a universal monarchy."[124] And the plurality of nations, together with all the conflicts this engenders, is the vehicle of progress.

These insights of aesthetic and reflective judgment have no practical consequences for action. As far as action is concerned, there is no doubt that moral-practical reason within us pronounces the following irresistible veto: *There shall be no war.* . . . Thus it is no longer a question of whether perpetual peace is really possible or not, or whether we are not perhaps mistaken in our theoretical judgment if we assume that it is. On the contrary, we must simply act as if it could really come about . . . even if the fulfillment of this pacific intention were forever to remain a pious hope . . . for it is our duty to do so.[125]

But these maxims for action do not nullify the aesthetic and reflective judgment. In other words: Even though Kant would always have acted for peace, he knew and kept in mind his judgment. Had he acted on the knowledge he had gained as a spectator, he would, in his own mind, have been criminal. Had he forgotten, because of this "moral duty," his insights as a spectator, he would have become what so many good men, involved and engaged in public affairs, tend to be—an idealistic fool.

Let me sum up: In the sections I have read to you, two very different factors were present almost everywhere—two factors closely interconnected in Kant's own mind but by no means otherwise. First, there was the position of the onlooker. What he saw counted most; he could discover a meaning in the course taken by events, a meaning that the actors ignored; and the existential ground for his insight was his disinterestedness, his nonparticipation, his noninvolvement. The onlooker's disinterested concern characterized the French Revolution as a great event. Second, there was the idea of progress, the hope for the future, where one judges the event according to the promise it holds for the generations to come. The two perspectives coincided in Kant's evaluation of the French Revolution, but this meant nothing as far as principles of action were concerned. But the two perspectives also somehow coincided in Kant's evaluation of war. War brings about progress—something no one can deny who knows how intimately the history of technology is connected with the history of wars. And war even brings about progress toward peace: war is so awful that, the more awful it gets, the more likely it is that men will become reasonable and work toward international agreements that will lead them eventually to peace. (Fate guides the willing ones, it drags the nonwilling along: *Fata ducunt volentem, trahunt nolentem.*)[126] But for Kant it is not fate; it is progress, a design behind men's backs, a ruse of nature or, later, a ruse of history.

The first of these notions—that only the spectator but never the actor knows what it is all about—is as old as the hills; it is, in fact, among the oldest, most decisive, notions of philosophy. The whole idea of the superiority of the contemplative way of life comes from this early insight that meaning (or truth) is revealed only to those who restrain themselves from acting. I shall give it to you in the simplest, least sophisticated form, in the form of a parable ascribed to Pythagoras:

> Life . . . is like a festival; just as some come to the festival to compete, some to ply their trade, but the best people come as spectators [theatai], so in life the slavish men go hunting for fame [doxa] or gain, the philosophers for truth.[127]

The data underlying this estimate are, first, that only the spectator occupies a position that enables him to see the whole; the actor, because he is part of the play, must enact his part—he is partial by definition. The spectator is impartial by definition—no part is assigned him. Hence, withdrawal from direct involvement to a standpoint outside the game is a condition sine qua non of all judgment. Second, what the actor is concerned with is doxa, fame—that is, the opinion of others (the word doxa means both "fame" and "opinion"). Fame comes about through the opinion of others. For the actor, the decisive question is thus how he appears to others (dokei hois allois); the actor is dependent on the opinion of the spectator; he is not autonomous (in Kant's language); he does not conduct himself according to an innate voice of reason but in accordance with what spectators would expect of him. The standard is the spectator. And this standard is autonomous.

Translating this into the terms of the philosophers, one arrives at the supremacy of the spectator's way of life, the bios theōrētikos (from theōrein, "to look at"). Here one escapes from the cave of opinions altogether and goes hunting for truth—no longer the truth of the games in the festival but the truth of things that are everlasting, that cannot be different from what they are (all human affairs can be different from what they actually are) and therefore are necessary. To the extent that one can actualize this withdrawal, one does what Aristotle called athanatizein, "to immortalize" (understood as an activity), and this one does with the divine part of one's soul. Kant's view is different: one withdraws also to the "theoretical," the onlooking, standpoint of the spectator, but this position is the position of the Judge. The whole terminology of Kant's philosophy is shot through with legal metaphors: it is the Tribunal of Reason before which the occurrences of the world appear. In either case: absorbed by the spectacle, I am outside it, I have given up the standpoint that determines my factual existence, with all its circumstantial, contingent conditions. Kant would have said: I have reached a general standpoint, the impartiality the Judge is supposed to exercise when he lays down his verdict. The Greeks would have said: we have given up the *dokei moi*, the it-seems-to-me, and the desire to seem to others; we have given up *doxa*, which is both opinion and fame.

There is joined to this old notion in Kant an altogether new one, the notion of progress, which actually provides the standard according to which one judges. The Greek spectator, whether at the festival of life or at the sight of the things that are everlasting, looks at and judges (finds the truth of) the cosmos of the particular event in its own terms, without relating it to any larger process in which it may or may not play a part. He was actually concerned with the individual event, the particular act. (Think of the Greek column, the absence of stairs, etc.) Its meaning did not depend on either causes or consequences. The story, once it had come to an end, contained the whole meaning. This is also true for Greek historiography, and it explains why Homer, Herodotus, and Thucydides can give the defeated enemy his due. The story may contain rules valid for future generations also, but it remains a single story. The last book, it seems, that is written in this spirit is Machiavelli's Florentine *Stories*, which you know under the misleading title of *The History of Florence*. The point is that, for Machiavelli, History was only the huge book that contained all the stories of men.

Progress as the standard by which to judge history somehow reverses the old principle that the meaning of a story reveals itself only at its end (*Nemo ante mortem beatus esse dici potest* [No one can be called blessed before his death]). In Kant, the story's or event's importance lies precisely not at its end but in its opening up new horizons for the future. It is the *hope* it contained for future generations that made the French Revolution such an important event. This feeling was widespread. Hegel, for whom the French Revolution also was the most important turning point, always describes it by metaphors like "a splendid rise of the sun," the "dawn," etc. It is a "world-historical" event because it contains the seeds of the future. The question here is: Who,

then, is the subject of the story? Not the men of the revolution;
they certainly did not have world history in mind. World history
can make sense only if

> something else results from the actions of men than what they
> intend and achieve, something else than they know or want.
> They accomplish their interest; but something else is accom-
> plished which was implied in it, which was not in the con-
> sciousness and the intentions of the actors. To give an anal-
> ogy, a man may set fire to the house of another out of re-
> venge. . . . [The] immediate action is to hold a small flame to a
> small part of a beam. . . . [What follows had not been in-
> tended:] a vast conflagration develops. . . . This result was
> neither part of the primary deed nor the intention of him
> who commenced it. . . . This example merely shows that in the
> immediate action something else may be involved than is con-
> sciously willed by the actor.[128]

These are Hegel's words, but they could have been written by
Kant. Yet there is a distinction between them, and it is twofold
and of great importance. In Hegel, it is Absolute Spirit that
reveals itself in the process, and it is this that the philosopher, at
the end of this revelation, can understand. In Kant, the subject
of world history is the human species itself. In Hegel, furthermore, the revelation of Absolute Spirit must come to an end
(history has an end in Hegel; the process is not infinite, hence
there is an end to the story, only this end needs many generations and centuries to come about); not man but Absolute Spirit
is finally disclosed, and the greatness of man is realized only
insofar as he is finally able to understand. But in Kant, progress
is perpetual; there is never an end to it. Hence, there is no end to
history. (In Hegel, as well as Marx, the notion that there is an
end to history is decisive; for it implies the inevitable question
What, if anything, is going to happen after this end has come
about?—leaving apart the rather obvious inclination of each
generation to believe that this eschatological end will come about
in its own lifetime. As Kojève rightly put it, driving to its inherent extreme the part of Hegel that influenced Marx: "After the
end of history, man can do nothing but perpetually rethink the
historical process which has been completed."[129] In Marx himself, on the other hand, the classless society and the realm of
freedom, based on abundance, will result in everyone's indulg-
ing in some sort of hobby.)

To come back to Kant: The subject that corresponds to world

history is the human species. The design of nature is to develop all of mankind's capabilities—mankind being understood as one of nature's animal species, with this decisive difference: Species in animals "means nothing more than the characteristics in virtue of which all individuals must directly agree with one another."[130] It is altogether different with the human species. By it,

> we understand the totality of a series of generations proceeding into infinity (the indeterminable). . . . [This] line of descent ceaselessly approaches its concurrent destination. . . . [It] is asymptotic in all its parts to this line of destiny, and on the whole coincides with it. In other words, no single member in all of these generations of the human race, but only the species, fully achieves its destination. . . . The philosopher would say that the destination of the human race in general is perpetual progress.[131]

From this, let us draw a few conclusions. History, we would say, is something built into the species man; the essence of man cannot be determined; and to Kant's own question, Why do men exist at all? the answer is: This question cannot be answered, for the "value of [their] existence" can be revealed "only in the whole," that is, never to any man or generation of men, since the process itself is perpetual.

Hence: In the center of Kant's moral philosophy stands the individual; in the center of his philosophy of history (or, rather, his philosophy of nature) stands the perpetual progress of the human race, or mankind. (Therefore: History from a general viewpoint.) The general viewpoint or standpoint is occupied, rather, by the spectator, who is a "world citizen" or, rather, a "world spectator." It is he who decides, by having an idea of the whole, whether, in any single, particular event, progress is being made.

Tenth Session

WE WERE TALKING ABOUT the clash between the spectator and the actor. The spectacle before the spectator—enacted, as it were, for his judgment—is history as a whole, and the true hero of this spectacle is mankind in the "series of generations proceeding" into some "infinity." This process has no end; the "destination of the human race is perpetual progress." In this process the capabilities of the human species are actualized, developed to "the highest pitch"—except that a highest one, in an absolute sense, does not exist. The ultimate destination, in the sense of eschatology, does not exist, but the two chief aims by which this progress is guided, though behind the backs of the actors, is *freedom*—in the simple and elementary sense that no one rules over his fellow men—and *peace* between nations as the condition for the unity of the human race. Perpetual progress toward freedom and peace, the latter guaranteeing free intercourse between all nations on the earth: these are the ideas of reason, without which the mere story of history would not make sense. It is the whole that gives meaning to the particulars if they are seen and judged by men endowed with reason. Men, though they are natural creatures and part of nature, transcend nature by virtue of a reason that asks: What is the purpose of nature? By producing one species with a faculty for asking such questions, nature has produced its own master. The human species is distinguished from all animal species not merely by its possession of speech and reason but because its faculties are capable of indeterminable development.

Up to now we have discussed the spectator in the singular, as Kant himself often does, and with good reason. First, there is the simple fact that one onlooker can behold many actors, who together offer the spectacle that unfolds before his eyes. Second, there is the whole weight of tradition, according to which the contemplative way of life presupposes withdrawal from the many; it singularizes one, as it were, because contemplation is a solitary business or, at least, can be carried on in solitude. You remember that, in the Parable of the Cave,[132] Plato says that its inhabitants, the many, who watch the shadow-play on the screen in front of them, are "chained by the legs and also by the neck, so that they cannot move and can see only what is in front of them, because the chains will not let them turn their heads"; hence also, they cannot communicate with one another about what they see. It is not only the philosopher returning from the light of the sky of Ideas who is a completely isolated figure. The spectators in the cave are also isolated, one from the other. Action, on the other hand, is never possible in solitude or isolation; one man alone needs, at the very least, the help of others to carry through whatever his enterprise may be. When the distinction between the two ways of life, the political (active) way and the philosophical (contemplative) way, is so construed as to render them mutually exclusive—as it is, for instance, in Plato's political philosophy—one gets an absolute distinction between the one who *knows* what is best to do and the others who, following his guidance or his commands, will carry it through. This is the gist of Plato's *Statesman:* the ideal ruler (*archōn*) does not act at all; he is the wise man who begins and knows the intended end of an action and therefore is the ruler. Hence, it would be entirely superfluous and even harmful for him to make his intentions known. We know that for Kant, on the contrary, publicness is the "transcendental principle" that should rule all action. Whatever act "stands in the need of publicity" in order not to defeat its own purpose is, you will remember, an act that combines politics and right. Kant cannot have the same notions as Plato about acting and mere judging or contemplating or knowing.

If you ask yourself where and who this public is that would give publicity to the intended act to begin with, it is quite obvious that in Kant's case it cannot be a public of actors or participators in government. The public he is thinking of is, of course, the reading public, and it is the weight of their opinion he is appealing to, not the weight of their votes. In the Prussia of the last decades of the eighteenth century—that is, a country under the rule of an absolute monarch, advised by a rather enlightened bureaucracy of civil servants, who, like the monarch, were completely separated from "the subjects"—there could be no truly public realm other than this reading and writing public. What was secret and unapproachable by definition was precisely the realm of government and administration. And if you read the essays from which I have quoted here, it should be clear that Kant could conceive of action only as acts of the powers-that-be (whatever they might happen to be)—that is, governmental acts; any actual action from the side of the subjects could consist only in conspiratorial activity, the acts and plots of secret societies. In other words, the alternative to established government is, for him, not revolution but a coup d'état. And a coup d'état, in contradistinction to a revolution, must indeed be prepared in secrecy, whereas revolutionary groups or parties have always been eager to make their goals public and to rally important sections of the population to their cause. Whether or not this strategy has ever brought about a revolution is another matter. But it is important to understand that Kant's condemnation of revolutionary action rests on a misunderstanding, because he conceives of it in terms of a coup d'état.

We are used to thinking about the difference between contemplation and action in terms of the relation between theory
and practice, and though it is true that Kant wrote an essay on
this matter, "On the Common Saying: 'This May be True in
Theory, But It Does Not Apply in Practice,'" it is also true, and is
best demonstrated by that essay, that he did not understand the
issue as we understand it. Kant's notion of practice is determined
by Practical Reason; and the *Critique of Practical Reason*, which
deals with neither judgment nor action, tells you all about it.
Judgment, arising out of "contemplative pleasure" and "inactive
delight," has no place in it.[133] In practical matters, not judgment
but will is decisive, and this will simply follows the maxim of
Reason. Even in the *Critique of Pure Reason* Kant starts his discussion of the "Pure Employment of Reason" with its *practical* implication, although he then provisionally "sets aside practical
[i.e., moral] ideas to consider reason only in its speculative . . . employment."[134] This speculation concerns the ultimate
destination of the individual, the ultimate of "the most sublime
questions."[135] Practical means moral in Kant, and it concerns the
individual *qua* individual. Its true opposite would be, not theory,
but speculation—the speculative use of reason. Kant's actual
theory in political affairs was the theory of perpetual progress
and a federal union of the nations in order to give the *idea* of
mankind a political reality. Whoever worked in this direction
was welcome. But these ideas, with whose help he reflected on
human affairs in general, are very different from the "wishful
participation bordering on enthusiasm" that caught the spectators of the French Revolution and "the exaltation [of] the uninvolved public" looking on in sympathy "without the least intention of assisting." In his opinion, it was precisely this sympathy that made the revolution a "phenomenon . . . not to be
forgotten"—or, in other words, that made it a public event of
world-historical significance. Hence: What constituted the appropriate public realm for this particular event were not the
actors but the acclaiming spectators.

Since Kant did not write his political philosophy, the best way
to find out what he thought about this matter is to turn to his
"Critique of Aesthetic Judgment," where, in discussing the production of art works in their relation to taste, which judges and
decides about them, he confronts an analogous problem. We—
for reasons we need not go into—are inclined to think that in
order to judge a spectacle you must first have the spectacle—that

the spectator is secondary to the actor; we tend to forget that no one in his right mind would ever put on a spectacle without being sure of having spectators to watch it. Kant is convinced that the world without man would be a desert, and a world without man means for him: without spectators. In his discussion of aesthetic judgment, Kant makes a distinction between genius and taste. Genius is required for the production of art works, while, for judging them, for deciding whether or not they are beautiful objects, "no more" (we would say, but not Kant) is required than taste. "For judging of beautiful objects *taste* is required . . . , for their production *genius* is required."[136] Genius, according to Kant, is a matter of productive imagination and originality, taste a mere matter of judgment. He raises the question, which of the two is the "more noble" faculty—which is the condition *sine qua non* "to which one has to look in the judging of art as beautiful art?"[137]—assuming, of course, that most of the judges of beauty lack the faculty of productive imagination, which is called genius, but that the few who are endowed with genius do not lack the faculty of taste. And the answer is:

> Abundance and originality of ideas are less necessary to beauty than the accordance of the imagination in its freedom with the conformity to law of the understanding [which is called taste]. For all the abundance of the former produces in lawless freedom nothing but nonsense; on the other hand, the judgment is the faculty by which it is adjusted to the understanding.
>
> Taste, like the judgment in general, is the discipline (or training) of genius; it clips its wings . . . , gives guidance . . . , brings clearness and order [into the thoughts of genius;] it makes the ideas susceptible of being permanently and generally assented to, and capable of being followed by others, and of an ever progressing culture. If, then, in the conflict of these two properties in a product something must be sacrificed, it should be rather on the side of genius.[138]

Kant allows this subordination of genius to taste even though without genius nothing for judgment to judge would exist. But Kant says explicitly that "for beautiful art . . . *imagination, intellect, spirit,* and *taste* are required," and he adds, in a note, that "the three former faculties are united by means of the fourth," that is, by taste—i.e., by judgment.[139] Spirit, moreover—a special faculty apart from reason, intellect, and imagination—enables the genius to find an expression for the ideas "by means of which the subjective state of mind brought about by them . . . can be communicated to others."[140] In other words, spirit—namely, that which inspires the genius and only him and which "no science can teach and no industry can learn"—consists in expressing 'the ineffable element in the state of mind [*Gemütszustand*]" that certain representations arouse in all of us but for which we have no words and would therefore be unable, without the help of genius, to communicate to one another; it is the proper task of genius to make this state of mind "generally communicable."[141] The faculty that guides this communicability is taste, and taste or judgment is not the privilege of genius. The condition *sine qua non* for the existence of beautiful objects is communicability; the judgment of the spectator creates the space without which no such objects could appear at all. The public realm is constituted by the critics and the spectators, not by the actors or the makers. And this critic and spectator sits in every actor and fabricator; without this critical, judging faculty the doer or maker would be so isolated from the spectator that he would not even be perceived. Or, to put it another way, still in Kantian terms: the very originality of the artist (or the very novelty of the actor) depends on his making himself understood by those who are not artists (or actors). And while one can speak of a genius in the singular because of his originality, one can never speak, as Pythagoras did, in the same way of *the* spectator. Spectators exist only in the plural. The spectator is not involved in the act, but he is always involved with fellow spectators. He does not share the faculty of genius, originality, with the maker or the faculty of novelty with the actor; the faculty they have in common is the faculty of judgment.

As far as making is concerned, this insight is at least as old as Latin (as distinguished from Greek) antiquity. We find it expressed for the first time in Cicero's *On the Orator*:

> For everybody discriminates [*dijudicare*], distinguishes between right and wrong in matters of art and proportion by some silent sense without any knowledge of art and proportion: and while they can do this in the case of pictures and statues, in other such works, for whose understanding nature has given them less equipment, they display this discrimination much more in judging the rhythms and pronunciations of words, since these are rooted [*infixa*] in common sense, and of such things nature has willed that no one should be altogether unable to sense and experience them [*expertus*].[142]

And he goes on to notice that it is truly marvelous and remarkable

> how little difference there is between the learned and the
> ignorant in judging, while there is the greatest difference in
> making.[143]

Kant, quite in the same vein, remarks in his *Anthropology* that
insanity consists in having lost this common sense that enables us
to judge as spectators; and the opposite of it is a *sensus privatus,* a
private sense, which he also calls "logical *Eigensinn,*"[144] implying
that our logical faculty, the faculty that enables us to draw conclusions from premises, could indeed function without communication—except that then, namely, if insanity has caused the
loss of common sense, it would lead to insane results precisely
because it has separated itself from the experience that can be
valid and validated only in the presence of others.

The most surprising aspect of this business is that common
sense, the faculty of judgment and of discriminating between
right and wrong, should be based on the sense of taste. Of our
five senses, three clearly give us objects of the external world and
therefore are easily communicable. Sight, hearing, and touch
deal directly and, as it were, objectively with objects; through
these senses objects are identifiable and can be shared with
others—can be expressed in words, talked about, etc. Smell and
taste give inner sensations that are entirely private and in-
communicable; what I taste and what I smell cannot be expressed in words at all. They seem to be private senses by definition. Moreover, the three objective senses have this in common:
they are capable of *re*presentation, of making present something
that is absent. I can, for example, recall a building, a melody,
the touch of velvet. This faculty—which in Kant is called
Imagination—is possessed by neither taste nor smell. On the
other hand, they are quite clearly the discriminatory senses: one
can withhold judgment from what one sees and, though less easily,
one can withhold judgment from what one hears or touches.
But in matters of taste or smell, the it-pleases-or-displeases-me is
immediate and overwhelming. And pleasure or displeasure,
again, are entirely idiosyncratic. Why then should taste—not beginning with Kant but ever since Gracián—be elevated to and
become the vehicle of the mental faculty of judgment? And
judgment, in turn—that is, not the judgment that is simply cognitive and resides in the senses that give us the objects we have in

common with all living things that have the same sensual equipment, but judgment between right and wrong—why should this be based on this *private* sense? Isn't it true that when it comes to matters of taste we are so little able to communicate that we cannot even dispute about them? *De gustibus non disputandum est.* The solution to this riddle is: Imagination. Imagination, the ability to make present what is absent, transforms the objects of the objective senses into "sensed" objects, as though they were objects of an inner sense. This happens by reflecting not on an object but on its representation. The represented object now arouses one's pleasure or displeasure, not direct perception of the object. Kant calls this "the operation of reflection."[145]

Eleventh Session

LET ME REPEAT, to remind you of what we were talking about before the vacation: We found that in Kant the common distinction or antagonism between theory and practice in political matters is the distinction between the spectator and the actor, and to our surprise we saw that the spectator had precedence: what counted in the French Revolution, what made it a world-historical event, a phenomenon not to be forgotten, were not the deeds and misdeeds of the actors but the opinions, the enthusiastic approbation, of spectators, of persons who themselves were not involved. We also saw that these uninvolved and non-participating spectators—who, as it were, made the event at home in the history of mankind and thus for all future action—*were* involved with one another (in contradistinction to the Pythagorean spectator at the Olympic games or the spectators in the Platonic cave, who could not communicate with one another). This much we got from Kant's political writings; but in order to understand this position we turned to the *Critique of Judgment,* and there we found that Kant was confronting a similar or analogous situation, the relation between the artist, the maker, or the genius and his audience. Again the question arose for Kant: Who is the more noble, and which is the more noble quality, to know how to make or to know how to judge? We saw that this was an old question, one that Cicero had already raised, namely, that everyone seems to be able to discriminate between right and wrong in matters of art but that very few are capable of making them; and Cicero said that this judging was done by a "silent sense"—meaning, probably, a sense that otherwise does not express itself.

This kind of judgment has, ever since Gracián, been called Taste, and we recalled that the phenomenon of taste was what actually led Kant to produce his *Critique of Judgment;* in fact, as late as 1787, he still called it a Critique of Taste. This then led us to ask ourselves why the mental phenomenon of Judgment was derived from the sense of taste and not from the more objective senses, especially the most objective of them, the sense of sight. We mentioned that taste and smell are the most private of the senses; that is, they sense not an object but a sensation, and this sensation is not object-bound and cannot be recollected. (You can recognize the smell of a rose or the taste of a particular dish if you sense it again, but in the absence of the rose or the food you cannot have it present as you can any sight you have ever seen or any melody you have ever heard, even though they are absent; in other words, these are senses that cannot be *re*presented.) At the same time, we saw why taste rather than any of the other senses became the vehicle for judgment; it was because only taste and smell are discriminatory by their very nature and because only these senses relate to the particular *qua* particular, whereas all objects given to the objective senses share their properties with other objects, that is, they are not unique. Moreover, the it-pleases-or-displeases-me is overwhelmingly present in taste and smell. It is immediate, unmediated by any thought or reflection. These senses are *subjective* because the very objectivity of the seen or heard or touched thing is annihilated in them or at least is not present; they are *inner* senses because the food we taste is inside ourselves, and so, in a way, is the smell of the rose. And the it-pleases-or-displeases-me is almost identical with an it-agrees-or-disagrees-with-me. The point of the matter is: I am directly affected. For this very reason, there can be no dispute about right or wrong here. *De gustibus non disputandum est*—there can be no dispute about matters of taste. No argument can persuade me to like oysters if I do not like them. In other words, the disturbing thing about matters of taste is that they are not communicable.

The solution to these riddles can be indicated by the names of two other faculties: *imagination* and *common sense.*

Imagination, that is, the faculty of having present what is absent,[146] transforms an object into something I do not have to be directly confronted with but that I have in some sense internalized, so that I now can be affected by it as though it were given to me by a nonobjective sense. Kant says: "That is beautiful which pleases in the mere act of judging it."[147] That is: It is not important whether or not it pleases in perception; what pleases merely in perception is gratifying but not beautiful. It pleases in representation, for now the imagination has prepared it so that I can reflect on it. This is "the operation of reflection." Only what touches, affects, one in representation, when one can no longer be affected by immediate presence—when one is uninvolved, like the spectator who was uninvolved in the actual doings of the French Revolution—can be judged to be right or wrong, important or irrelevant, beautiful or ugly, or something in between. One then speaks of judgment and no longer of taste because, though it still affects one like a matter of taste, one now has, by means of representation, established the proper distance, the remoteness or uninvolvedness or disinterestedness, that is requisite for approbation and disapprobation, for evaluating something at its proper worth. By removing the object, one has established the conditions for impartiality.

As for common sense: Kant was very early aware that there was something nonsubjective in what seems to be the most private and subjective sense. This awareness is expressed as follows: there is the fact that, in matters of taste, "the beautiful, interests [us] only [when we are] in *society*. . . . A man abandoned by himself on a desert island would adorn neither his hut nor his person. . . . [Man] is not contented with an object if he cannot feel satisfaction in it in common with others."[148] Or: "We are ashamed if our taste does not agree with others," whereas we despise ourselves when we cheat at play but are ashamed only when we get caught. Or: "In matters of taste we must renounce ourselves in favor of others" or in order to please others (*Wir müssen uns gleichsam anderen zu gefallen entsagen*).[149] Finally, and most radically: "In Taste egoism is overcome"; that is, we are "considerate," in the original meaning of the word. We must overcome our special subjective conditions for the sake of others. In other words, the nonsubjective element in the nonobjective senses is intersubjectivity. (You must be alone in order to think; you need company to enjoy a meal.)

Judgment, and especially judgments of taste, always reflects upon others and their taste, takes their possible judgments into account. This is necessary because I am human and cannot live outside the company of men. I judge as a member of this community and not as a member of a supersensible world, perhaps inhabited with beings endowed with reason but not with the same sense apparatus; as such, I obey a law given to myself regardless of what others may think of the matter. This law is self-evident and compelling in and by itself. The basic other-directedness of judgment and taste seems to stand in the greatest possible opposition to the very nature, the absolutely idiosyncratic nature, of the sense itself. Hence we may be tempted to conclude that the faculty of judgment is wrongly derived from this sense. Kant, being very aware of all the implications of this derivation, remains convinced that it is a correct one. And the most plausible thing in his favor is his observation, entirely correct, that the true opposite of the Beautiful is not the Ugly but "that which excites *disgust.*"¹⁵⁰ And do not forget that Kant originally planned to write a Critique of Moral Taste, so that the phenomenon of the beautiful is, so to speak, what is left of his early observations about these phenomena of judgment.

Twelfth Session

THERE ARE TWO MENTAL OPERATIONS in judgment. There is the operation of the imagination, in which one judges objects that are no longer present, that are removed from immediate sense perception and therefore no longer affect one directly, and yet, though the object is removed from one's outward senses, it now becomes an object for one's inner senses. When one represents something to oneself that is absent, one closes, as it were, those senses by which objects in their objectivity are given to one. The sense of taste is a sense in which one, as it were, senses oneself; it is an inner sense. Hence: the *Critique of Judgment* grows out of the Critique of Taste. This operation of imagination prepares the object for "the operation of reflection." And this second operation—the operation of reflection—is the actual activity of judging something.

    This twofold operation establishes the most important condition for all judgments, the condition of impartiality, of "disinterested delight." By closing one's eyes one becomes an impartial, not a directly affected, spectator of visible things. The blind poet. Also: by making what one's external senses perceived into an object for one's inner sense, one compresses and condenses the manifold of the sensually given; one is in a position to "see" by the eyes of the mind, i.e., to see the whole that gives meaning to the particulars. The advantage the spectator has is that he sees the play as a whole, while each of the actors knows only his part or, if he should judge from the perspective of acting, only the part of the whole that concerns him. The actor is partial by definition.

The question that now arises is this: What are the standards of the operation of reflection? The operation of imagination has made the absent immediately present to one's inner sense, and this inner sense is discriminatory by definition: it says it-pleases or it-displeases. It is called taste because, like taste, it *chooses*. But this choice is itself subject to still another choice: one can approve or disapprove of the very fact of *pleasing:* this too is subject to "approbation or disapprobation." Kant gives examples: "The joy of a needy but well-meaning man at becoming the heir of an affectionate but penurious father"; or, conversely, "a deep grief may satisfy the person experiencing it (the sorrow of a widow at the death of her excellent husband); or . . . a gratification can in addition please (as in the sciences that we pursue); or a grief (e.g. hatred, envy, revenge) can, moreover, displease."[151] All these approbations and disapprobations are afterthoughts; at the time you are doing scientific research you may be vaguely aware that you are happy doing it, but only later, in reflecting on it, when you are no longer busy doing whatever you were doing, will you be able to have this additional "pleasure": of *approving* it. In this additional pleasure it is no longer the object that pleases but *that* we judge it to be pleasing. If we relate this to the whole of nature or the world, we can say: We are pleased that the world or nature pleases us. The very act of approbation pleases, the very act of disapprobation displeases. Hence the question: How does one choose between approbation and disapprobation? One criterion is easily guessed if one considers the examples given above; it is the criterion of communicability or publicness. One is not overeager to express joy at the death of a father or feelings of hatred and envy; one will, on the other hand, have no compunctions about announcing that one enjoys doing scientific work, and one will not hide grief at the death of an excellent husband.

The criterion, then, is communicability, and the standard of deciding about it is common sense.

Critique of Judgment, § 39:
"Of the Communicability of a Sensation"

It is true that the sensation of the senses is "generally communicable because we can assume that everyone has senses like our own. But this cannot be presupposed of any single sensation."

These sensations are private; also, no judgment is involved: we are merely passive, we react, we are not spontaneous, as we are when we imagine something at will or reflect on it.

At the opposite pole we find moral judgments. These, according to Kant, are necessary; they are dictated by practical reason. They might be communicated, but this communication is secondary; even if they could not be communicated, they would remain valid.

We have, third, judgments of, or pleasure in, the beautiful: "this pleasure accompanies the ordinary apprehension [*Auffasung; not* "perception"] of an object by the imagination . . . by means of a procedure of the judgment which it must also exercise on behalf of the commonest experience." Some such judgment is in every experience we have with the world. This judgment is based on "that common and sound intellect [*gemeiner und gesunder Verstand*] which we have to presuppose in everyone." How does this "common sense" distinguish itself from the other senses, which we also have in common but which nevertheless do not guarantee agreement of sensations?

Critique of Judgment, § 40:
"Of Taste
as a Kind of *Sensus Communis*"

The term is changed. The term "common sense" meant a sense like our other senses—the same for everyone in his very privacy. By using the Latin term, Kant indicates that here he means something different: an extra sense—like an extra mental capability (German: *Menschenverstand*)—that fits us into a community. The "common understanding of men . . . is the very least to be expected from anyone claiming the name of man." It is the capability by which men are distinguished from animals and from gods. It is the very humanity of man that is manifest in this sense.

The *sensus communis* is the specifically human sense because communication, i.e., speech, depends on it. To make our needs known, to *express* fear, joy, etc., we would not need speech. Gestures would be enough, and sounds would be a good enough substitute for gestures if one needed to bridge long distances. Communication is not expression. Thus: "The only general symptom of insanity is the loss of the *sensus communis* and the logical stubbornness in insisting on one's own sense (*sensus privatus*), which [in an insane person] is substituted for it" ["Das einzige allgemeine Merkmal der Verücktheit ist der Verlust des Gemeinsinnes (*sensus communis*) und der dagegen eintretende logische Eigensinn (*sensus privatus*)"].[152] The insane person has not lost his powers of expression to make his needs manifest and known to others.

[U]nder the *sensus communis* we must include the idea of a sense *common to all*, i.e., of a faculty of judgment which, in its reflection, takes account (*a priori*) of the mode of representation of all other men in thought, in order, *as it were*, to compare its judgment with the collective reason of humanity. . . . This is done by comparing our judgment with the possible rather than the actual judgments of others, and by putting ourselves in the place of any other man, by abstracting from the limitations which contingently attach to our own judgment. . . . Now this operation of reflection seems perhaps too artificial to be attributed to the faculty called *common* sense, but it only appears so when expressed in abstract formulae. In itself there is nothing more natural than to abstract from charm or emotion if we are seeking a judgment that is to serve as a universal rule.[153]

After this, follow the maxims of this *sensus communis:* Think for oneself (the maxim of enlightenment); Put oneself in thought in the place of everyone else (the maxim of the enlarged mentality); and, the maxim of consistency, Be in agreement with oneself ("mit sich selbst Einstimmung denken").[154]

These are not matters of cognition; truth compels, one doesn't need any "maxims." Maxims apply and are needed only for matters of opinion and in judgments. And just as, in moral matters, one's maxim of conduct testifies to the quality of one's will, so the maxims of judgment testify to one's "turn of thought" (*Denkungsart*) in the worldly matters that are ruled by the community sense:

However small may be the area or the degree to which a man's natural gifts reach, yet it indicates a man of *enlarged thought* if he disregards the subjective private conditions of his own judgment, by which so many others are confined, and reflects upon it from a *general standpoint* (which he can only determine by placing himself at the standpoint of others).[155]

After this we find a clear distinction between what usually is called common sense and *sensus communis*. Taste is this "community sense" (*gemeinschaftlicher Sinn*), and sense means here "the effect of a reflection upon the mind." This reflection affects me

as though it were a sensation, and precisely one of taste, the
discriminatory, choosing sense. "We could even define taste as
the faculty of judging of that which makes generally communicable, without the mediation of a concept, our feeling [like sen-
sation] in a given representation [not perception]."[156]

> Taste is then the faculty of judging *a priori* of the communica-
> bility of feelings that are bound up with a given representa-
> tion.... If we could assume that the mere general com-
> municability of a feeling must carry in itself an interest for us
> with it ... we should be able to explain why the feeling in the
> judgment of taste comes to be imputed to everyone, so to
> speak, as a duty.[157]

Thirteenth Session

WE NOW CONCLUDE our discussion of common sense in its very
special Kantian meaning, according to which common sense is
community sense, *sensus communis*, as distinguished from *sensus
privatus*. This *sensus communis* is what judgment appeals to in
everyone, and it is this possible appeal that gives judgments their
special validity. The it-pleases-or-displeases-me, which as a feeling seems so utterly private and noncommunicative, is actually
rooted in this community sense and is therefore open to communication once it has been transformed by reflection, which
takes all others and their feelings into account. The validity of
these judgments never has the validity of cognitive or scientific
propositions, which are not judgments, properly speaking. (If
one says, "The sky is blue" or "Two and two are four," one is not
"judging"; one is saying what is, compelled by the evidence
either of one's senses or one's mind.) Similarly, one can never
compel anyone to agree with one's judgments—"This is beautiful" or "This is wrong" (Kant does not believe that moral judgments are the product of reflection and imagination, hence they
are not judgments strictly speaking); one can only "woo" or
"court" the agreement of everyone else. And in this persuasive
activity one actually appeals to the "community sense." In other
words, when one judges, one judges as a member of a community. It is in "the nature of judgment, whose right use is so
necessarily and so generally requisite, that by the name of 'sound
understanding' [common sense in its usual meaning] nothing
else but this faculty is meant."[158]

Critique of Judgment, §41:
"Of the Empirical Interest in the Beautiful"

We turn now, briefly, to §41 of the *Critique of Judgment.* We saw
that an "enlarged mentality" is the condition *sine qua non* of right
judgment; one's community sense makes it possible to enlarge
one's mentality. Negatively speaking, this means that one is able
to abstract from private conditions and circumstances, which, as
far as judgment is concerned, limit and inhibit its exercise. Private conditions condition us; imagination and reflection enable
us to *liberate* ourselves from them and to attain that relative
impartiality that is the specific virtue of judgment. The less
idiosyncratic one's taste is, the better it can be communicated;
communicability is again the touchstone. Impartiality in Kant is
called "disinterestedness," the disinterested delight in the Beautiful. Disinterestedness is actually implied in the very words
beautiful and ugly, as it is not in the words right and wrong. If,
therefore, §41 speaks of an "Interest in the Beautiful," it actually
speaks of having an "interest" in disinterestedness. Interest here
refers to usefulness. If you look at nature, there are many natural objects in which you have an immediate interest because they
are useful for the life process. The problem, as Kant sees it, is
the superabundance of nature; there are so many things that
seem literally good for nothing except that their form is
beautiful—for instance, crystals. Because we can call something
beautiful, we have a *"pleasure in its existence,"* and that is "wherein
all interest consists." (In one of his reflections in the Notebooks,
Kant remarks that the Beautiful teaches us to "love without
self-interest [*ohne Eigennutz*].") And the peculiar characteristic of
this interest is that it "interests only in society":

> If we admit the impulse to society as natural to man, and his
> fitness for it, and his propension toward it, i.e., *sociability,* as a
> requisite for man as a being destined for society, and so as a
> property belonging to *being human and humaneness* [*Humani-
> tät*], we cannot escape from regarding taste as a faculty for
> judging everything in respect of which we can communicate
> our *feeling* to all other men, and so as a means of furthering
> that which everyone's natural inclination desires.[159]

In "Conjectural Beginning of Human History" Kant states that
"the highest end intended for man is sociability,"[160] and this
sounds as though sociability is a goal to be pursued through the
course of civilization. We find here, on the contrary, sociability as

the very origin, not the goal, of man's humanity; that is, we find that sociability is the very essence of men insofar as they are of this world only. This is a radical departure from all those theories that stress human interdependence as dependence on our fellow men for our *needs* and *wants*. Kant stresses that at least one of our *mental faculties*, the faculty of judgment, presupposes the presence of others. And this mental faculty is not just what we terminologically call judgment; bound up with it is the notion that "feelings and emotions [*Empfindungen*] are regarded as of worth only insofar as they can be generally communicated"; that is, bound up with judgment is our whole soul apparatus, so to speak. Communicability obviously depends on the enlarged mentality; one can communicate only if one is able to think from the other person's standpoint; otherwise one will never meet him, never speak in such a way that he understands. By communicating one's feelings, one's pleasures and disinterested delights, one tells one's *choices* and one chooses one's company: "I would rather be wrong with Plato than right with the Pythagoreans."[161] Finally, the larger the scope of those to whom one can communicate, the greater is the worth of the object:

> [A]lthough the pleasure which everyone has in such an object is inconsiderable [that is, so long as he does not share it] and in itself without any marked interest, yet the idea of its general communicability increases its worth in an almost infinite degree.[162]

At this point, the *Critique of Judgment* joins effortlessly Kant's deliberation about a united mankind, living in eternal peace. What interests Kant in the abolition of war and makes him an odd kind of pacifist is not the elimination of conflict, not even the elimination of the cruelty, the bloodshed, the atrocities of warfare. It is, as he sometimes even grudgingly concludes (grudgingly, because men could become like sheep; there is something sublime in the sacrifice of life; etc.), the necessary condition for the greatest possible enlargement of the enlarged mentality:

> [If] everyone expects and requires from everyone else this reference to general communication [of pleasure, of disinterested delight, then we have reached a point where it is as if there existed] an original compact, dictated by mankind itself.[163]

This compact, according to Kant, would be a mere idea, reg-

ulating not just our reflections on these matters but actually
inspiring our actions. It is by virtue of this idea of mankind,
present in every single man, that men are human, and they can
be called civilized or humane to the extent that this idea becomes
the principle not only of their judgments but of their actions. It
is at this point that actor and spectator become united; the
maxim of the actor and the maxim, the "standard," according to
which the spectator judges the spectacle of the world, become
one. The, as it were, categorical imperative for action could read
as follows: Always act on the maxim through which this original
compact can be actualized into a general law. It is from this
viewpoint, and not just from love of peace, that the treatise
Perpetual Peace was written, that the "Preliminary Articles" of the
first section and the "Definitive Articles" of the second section
were spelled out. Among the former, the most important and
also the most original is the sixth:

> No state shall, during war, permit such acts of hostility which
> would make mutual confidence in the subsequent peace im-
> possible.[164]

Among the latter, it is the third that actually follows directly
from sociability and communicability:

> The law of world citizenship shall be limited to conditions of
> universal hospitality.[165]

If such an original compact of mankind exists, then a "right of
temporary sojourn, a right to associate," is one of the inalienable
human rights. Men

> have it by virtue of their common possession of the earth,
> where, as a globe, they cannot infinitely disperse and hence
> must finally tolerate the presence of each other. . . . [For] the
> common right to the face of the earth . . . belongs to human
> beings generally. . . . [All of which can be proved negatively by
> the fact] that a violation of rights in one place is felt through-
> out the world, [from which Kant concluded that] the idea of a
> law of world citizenship is no high-flown or exaggerated no-
> tion.[166]

To come back to what we said before: One judges always as a
member of a community, guided by one's community sense,
one's *sensus communis*. But in the last analysis, one is a member of
a world community by the sheer fact of being human; this is
one's "cosmopolitan existence." When one judges and when one

acts in political matters, one is supposed to take one's bearings from the idea, not the actuality, of being a world citizen and, therefore, also a *Weltbetrachter,* a world spectator.

In conclusion, I shall try to clear up some of the difficulties. The chief difficulty in judgment is that it is "the faculty of thinking the particular";[167] but to *think* means to generalize, hence it is the faculty of mysteriously combining the particular and the general. This is relatively easy if the general is given—as a rule, a principle, a law—so that the judgment merely subsumes the particular under it. The difficulty becomes great "if only the particular be given for which the general has to be found."[168] For the standard cannot be borrowed from experience and cannot be derived from outside. I cannot judge one particular by another particular; in order to determine its worth, I need a *tertium quid* or a *tertium comparationis,* something related to the two particulars and yet distinct from both. In Kant we find actually two altogether different solutions to this difficulty:

As a real *tertium comparationis,* two ideas appear in Kant on which one must reflect in order to arrive at judgments. The first, which appears in the political writings and, occasionally, in the *Critique of Judgment,* is the idea of an original compact of mankind as a whole, and derived from this idea is the notion of humanity, of what actually constitutes the humanness of human beings, living and dying in this world, on this earth that is a globe, which they inhabit in common, share in common, in the succession of generations. In the *Critique of Judgment* one also finds the idea of purposiveness. Every object, says Kant, as a particular, needing and containing the ground of its actuality in itself, has a purpose. The only objects that seem purposeless are aesthetic objects, on the one hand, and men, on the other. You cannot ask *quem ad finem?*—for what purpose?—since they are good for nothing. But we saw that the purposeless art objects, as well as the seemingly purposeless variety of nature, have the "purpose" of pleasing men, making them feel at home in the world. This can never be proved; but purposiveness is an idea by which to regulate one's reflections in one's reflective judgments.

But Kant's second, and I think by far more valuable, solution is *exemplary* validity. ("Examples are the go-cart of judgments.")[169] Let us see what this is. Every particular object—for instance, a table—has a corresponding concept by which we recognize the table as a table. This can be conceived of as a "Platonic" idea or Kantian schema; that is, one has before the eyes of one's mind a schematic or merely *formal table* shape to which every table somehow must conform. Or one proceeds, conversely, from the many tables one has seen in one's life, strips them of all secondary qualities, and the remainder is a table-in-general, containing the minimum properties common to all tables: the *abstract table*. One more possibility is left, and this enters into judgments that are not cognitions: one may encounter or think of some table that one judges to be the best possible table and take this table as the example of how tables actually should be: the *exemplary table* ("example" comes from *eximere*, "to single out some particular"). This exemplar is and remains a particular that in its very particularity reveals the generality that otherwise could not be defined. Courage is *like* Achilles. Etc.

We were talking about the partiality of the actor, who, because he is involved, never sees the meaning of the whole. This is true for all stories; Hegel is entirely right that philosophy, like the owl of Minerva, spreads its wings only when the day is over, at dusk. The same is not true for the beautiful or for any deed in itself. The beautiful is, in Kantian terms, an end in itself because all its possible meaning is contained within itself, without reference to others—without linkage, as it were, to other beautiful things. In Kant himself there is this contradiction: Infinite Progress is the law of the human species; at the same time, man's dignity demands that he be seen (every single one of us) in his particularity and, as such, be seen—but without any comparison and independent of time—as reflecting mankind in general. In other words, the very idea of progress—if it is more than a change in circumstances and an improvement of the world—contradicts Kant's notion of man's dignity. It is against human dignity to believe in progress. Progress, moreover, means that the story never has an end. The end of the story itself is in infinity. There is no point at which we might stand still and look back with the backward glance of the historian.

Imagination

Seminar on Kant's *Critique of Judgment,* given at the
New School for Social Research, Fall, 1970

[In these seminar notes Hannah Arendt elaborates the notion of exemplary validity, introduced on pages 76–77 of the Kant Lectures, by turning to Kant's analysis of Transcendental Imagination in the account of the Schematism in the first edition of the *Critique of Pure Reason.* Exemplary validity is of crucial importance, for it supplies the basis for a conception of political science centered on *particulars* (stories, historical examples), not *universals* (the concept of historical process; general laws of history). Arendt quotes Kant to the effect that what the schemata do for cognition, examples do for judgment (*Critique of Judgment,* §59). Without this important background concerning the Schematism from the first *Critique,* we lack a full appreciation of the role of imagination in representation and, therewith, in judgment. It would be a mistake to suppose that these pages on Imagination are on a *different* topic, of only passing relevance to judging. On the contrary, this seminar material, with its extended account of exemplary validity, relating it to the function of imagination in the Schematism, supplies an indispensable piece in the puzzle if we hope to reconstruct the full contours of Arendt's theory of judging.—R. B.]

I. Imagination, Kant says, is the faculty of making present what is absent, the faculty of re-presentation: "Imagination is the faculty of representing in *intuition* an object that is not itself present."[1] Or: "Imagination (*facultas imaginandi*) is a faculty of *perception* in the absence of an object."[2] To give the name "imagination" to this faculty of having present what is absent is natural enough. If I represent what is absent, I have an *image* in my mind—an image of something I have seen and now somehow reproduce. (In the *Critique of Judgment,* Kant sometimes calls this faculty "reproductive"—I represent what I have seen—to distinguish it from the "productive" faculty—the artistic faculty that produces something it has never seen. But productive imagination [genius] is never entirely productive. It produces, for instance, the centaur out of the given: the horse and the man.)

This sounds as though we are dealing with memory. But for Kant, imagination is the condition for memory, and a much more comprehensive faculty. In his *Anthropology* Kant puts memory, "the faculty to make present the *past,*" together with a "faculty of divination," which makes present the *future.* Both are faculties of "association," that is, of connecting the "no longer" and the "not yet" with the present; and "although they themselves are not perceptions, they serve to connect the perceptions in time."[3] Imagination does not need to be led by this temporal association; it can make present at will whatever it chooses.

What Kant calls the faculty of imagination, to make present to the mind what is absent from sense perception, has less to do with memory than with another faculty, one that has been known since the beginnings of philosophy. Parmenides (fragment 4) called it *nous* (that faculty "through which you look steadfastly at things which are present though they are absent"),[4] and by this he meant that Being is never present, does not present itself to the senses. What is not present in the perception of things is the *it-is;* and the *it-is,* absent from the senses, is nevertheless present to the mind. Or Anaxagoras: *Opsis tōn adē-lōn ta phainomena,* "A glimpse of the nonvisible are the appearances."[5] To put this differently: by looking at appearances (given to intuition in Kant) one becomes aware of, gets a glimpse of, something that does not appear. This something is Being as such. Hence, metaphysics, the discipline that treats of what lies beyond physical reality and still, in a mysterious way, is given to the mind as the nonappearance in the appearances, becomes ontology, the science of Being.

II. The role of imagination for our cognitive faculties is perhaps the greatest discovery Kant made in the *Critique of Pure Reason.* For our purposes it is best to turn to the "Schematism of the Pure Concepts of Understanding."[6] To anticipate: the same faculty, imagination, which provides schemata for cognition, provides *examples* for judgment.

You will recall that in Kant there are the two stems of experience and knowledge: intuition (sensibility) and concepts (understanding). Intuition always *gives* us something particular; the concept makes this particular *known* to us. If I say: "this table," it is as though intuition says "this" and the understanding adds: "table." "This" relates only to this specific item; "table" identifies it and makes the object communicable.

Two questions arise. First, how do the two faculties come together? To be sure, the concepts of understanding enable the
mind to order the manifold of the sensations. But where does
the synthesis, their working together, spring from? Second, is
this concept, "table," a concept at all? Is it not perhaps also a kind
of image? So that some sort of imagination is present in the
intellect as well? The answer is: "Synthesis of a manifold . . . is
what first gives rise to knowledge. . . . [It] gathers the elements
for knowledge, and unites them into a certain content"; this
synthesis "is the mere result of the faculty of imagination, a blind
but indispensable function of the soul, without which we should
have no knowledge *whatsoever,* but of which we are scarcely ever
conscious."[7] And the way imagination produces the synthesis is
by "providing an *image for a concept.*"[8] Such an image is called a
"schema."

> The two extremes, namely sensibility and understanding,
> must be brought into connection with each other by
> means . . . of imagination, because otherwise the former,
> though indeed yielding appearances, would supply no objects
> of empirical knowledge, hence no experience.[9]

Here Kant calls upon imagination to provide the connection
between the two faculties, and in the first edition of the *Critique
of Pure Reason* he calls the faculty of imagination "the faculty of
synthesis in general [*überhaupt*]." At other places where he
speaks directly of the "schematism" involved in our understanding, he calls it "an art concealed in the depths of the human
soul"[10] (i.e., we have a kind of "intuition" of something that is
never present), and by this he suggests that imagination is actually the common root of the other cognitive faculties, that is, it is
the "common, but to us unknown, root" of sensibility and understanding,[11] of which he speaks in the Introduction to the *Critique
of Pure Reason* and which, in its last chapter, without naming the
faculty, he mentions again.[12]

III. *Schema:* The point of the matter is that without a "schema"
one can never recognize anything. When one says: "this table,"
the general "image" of table is present in one's mind, and one
recognizes that the "this" is a table, something that shares its
qualities with many other such things though it is itself an individual, particular thing. If I recognize a house, this perceived
house also includes how a house in general looks. This is what

Plato called the *eidos*—the general form—of a house, which is
never given to the natural senses but only to the eyes of the
mind. Since, strictly speaking, it is not given even to "the eyes of
the mind," it is something *like* an "image" or, better, a "schema."
Whenever one draws or builds a house, one draws or builds a
particular house, not the house as such. Still, one could not do it
without having this schema or *eidos* before the eye of one's mind.
Or, as Kant says: "No image could ever be adequate to the concept of triangle in general. It would never attain that universality
of the concept which renders it valid of all triangles, whether
right-angled, obtuse-angled, or acute-angled; . . . the schema of
the triangle can exist nowhere but in thought."[13] Yet, though it
exists in thought only, it is a kind of "image"; it is not a product
of thought, nor is it given to sensibility; and least of all is it the
product of an abstraction from sensibly given data. It is something beyond or between thought and sensibility; it belongs to
thought insofar as it is outwardly invisible, and it belongs to
sensibility insofar as it is something *like* an image. Kant therefore
sometimes calls imagination "one of the original sources . . . of all
experience," and says that it cannot itself "be derived from any
other faculty of the mind."[14]

One more example: "The concept 'dog' signifies a rule according to which my imagination can delineate the figure of a
four-footed animal in a general manner [but as soon as the
figure is delineated on paper it is again a particular animal!],
without limitation to any single determinate figure such as experience, or any possible image that I can represent *in concreto,*
actually presents."[15] This is the "art concealed in the depths of
the human soul, whose real modes of activity nature is hardly
likely ever to allow us to discover and to have open to our
gaze."[16] Kant says that the image—for instance, the George
Washington Bridge—is the product "of the empirical faculty of
reproductive imagination; the schema [bridge] . . . is a product . . . of pure *a priori* imagination . . . through which images
themselves first become possible."[17] In other words: if I did not
have the faculty of "schematizing," I could not have images.

IV. For us, the following points are decisive.

1. In perception of this particular table there is contained
"table" as such. Hence, no perception is possible without imagination. Kant remarks that "psychologists have hitherto failed to

realize that imagination is a necessary ingredient of perception itself."[18]

2. The schema "table" is valid for all particular tables. Without it, we would be surrounded by a manifold of objects of which we could say only "this" and "this" and "this." Not only would no knowledge be possible, but communication—"Bring me a table" (no matter which)—would be impossible.

3. Hence: Without the ability to say "table," we could never communicate. We can describe the George Washington Bridge because we all know: "bridge." Suppose someone comes along who does not know "bridge," and there is no bridge to which I could point and utter the word. I would then draw an image of the schema of a bridge, which of course is already a particular bridge, just to remind him of some schema known to him, such as "transition from one side of the river to the other."

In other words: What makes particulars *communicable* is (a) that in perceiving a particular we have in the back of our minds (or in the "depths of our souls") a "schema" whose "shape" is characteristic of many such particulars *and* (b) that this schematic shape is in the back of the minds of many different people. These schematic shapes are products of the imagination, although "no schema can ever be brought into any image whatsoever."[19] All single agreements or disagreements presuppose that we are talking about the same thing—that we, who are many, agree, come together, on something that is one and the same for us all.

4. The *Critique of Judgment* deals with reflective judgments as distinguished from determinant ones. Determinant judgments subsume the particular under a general rule; reflective judgments, on the contrary, "derive" the rule from the particular. In the schema, one actually "perceives" some "universal" in the particular. One sees, as it were, the schema "table" by recognizing the table as table. Kant hints at this distinction between determinant and reflective judgments in the *Critique of Pure Reason* by drawing a distinction between "subsuming under a concept" and "bringing to a concept."[20]

5. Finally, our sensibility seems to need imagination not only as an aid to knowledge but in order to recognize sameness in the manifold. As such, it is the condition of all knowledge: the "synthesis of imagination, prior to apperception, is the ground of the possibility of all knowledge, especially of experience."[21] As

such, imagination "determines the sensibility *a priori*," i.e., it is inherent in all sense perceptions. Without it, there would be neither the objectivity of the world—that it can be known—nor any possibility of communication—that we can talk about it.

V. The importance of the schema for our purposes is that sensibility and understanding meet in producing it through imagination. In the *Critique of Pure Reason* imagination is at the service of the intellect; in the *Critique of Judgment* the intellect is "at the service of imagination."[22]

In the *Critique of Judgment* we find an analogy to the "schema": the *example*.[23] Kant accords to examples the same role in judgments that the intuitions called schemata have for experience and cognition. Examples play a role in both reflective and determinant judgments, that is, whenever we are concerned with particulars. In the *Critique of Pure Reason*—where we read that "judgment is a peculiar talent which can be practiced only, and cannot be taught" and that "its lack no school can make good"[24]—they are called "the go-cart [*Gängelband*] of judgment."[25] In the *Critique of Judgment*, i.e., in the treatment of reflective judgments, where one does not subsume a particular under a concept, the example helps one in the same way in which the schema helped one to recognize the table as table. The examples lead and guide us, and the judgment thus acquires "exemplary validity."[26]

The example is the particular that contains in itself, or is supposed to contain, a concept or a general rule. How, for instance, is one able to judge, to evaluate, an act as courageous? When judging, one says spontaneously, without any derivations from general rules, "This man has courage." If one were a Greek, one would have in "the depths of one's mind" the example of Achilles. Imagination is again necessary: one must have Achilles present even though he certainly is absent. If we say of somebody that he is good, we have in the back of our minds the example of Saint Francis or Jesus of Nazareth. The judgment has exemplary validity to the extent that the example is rightly chosen. Or, to take another instance: in the context of French history I can talk about Napoleon Bonaparte as a particular man; but the moment I speak about Bonapartism I have made an example of him. The validity of this example will be restricted to those who possess the particular experience of Napoleon, either as his contemporaries or as the heirs to this particular historical tradition. Most concepts in the historical and political sciences are of this restricted nature; they have their origin in some particular historical incident, and we then proceed to make it "exemplary"—to see in the particular what is valid for more than one case.

PART TWO

Interpretive Essay

Hannah Arendt on Judging

Ronald Beiner

1. Judging: Resolution of an Impasse

JUDGING WAS TO HAVE SUCCEEDED *Thinking* and *Willing* as the third and concluding part of Hannah Arendt's final work, *The Life of the Mind*. But as Mary McCarthy, editor of the posthumous work, tells us in her Postface to the two published volumes, Arendt's sudden death came less than a week after she had completed the draft of *Willing*: "After her death, a sheet of paper was found in her typewriter, blank except for the heading 'Judging' and two epigraphs. Some time between the Saturday of finishing 'Willing' and the Thursday of her death, she must have sat down to confront the final section."[1] It can be maintained that, without the account of judging, our picture of *The Life of the Mind* is in a decisive respect incomplete. First of all, we have the testimony of Hannah Arendt's friend J. Glenn Gray that "she regarded judging to be her particular strength and in a real sense a hoped-for resolution of the impasse to which the reflections on willing seemed to lead her. As Kant's *Critique of Judgment* enabled him to break through some of the antinomies of the earlier critiques, so she hoped to resolve the perplexities of thinking and willing by pondering the nature of our capacity for judging."[2] It is not merely that the already completed accounts of two mental faculties were to be supplemented by a yet-to-be-provided third but, rather, that those two accounts themselves remain deficient without the promised synthesis in judging. Michael Denneny, commenting on Arendt's precursory lectures on thinking, willing, and judging, which he attended in 1966, offers a similar verdict: "The lectures on thinking (and conscience and consciousness) were brilliantly original and stimulating; those on the will, difficult and puzzling. And it became increasingly clear that the heart of the matter lay in judgment." Denneny adds that this involved a strange irony, for, "surprisingly, the discussion of this faculty was constantly postponed, and, in the end, it was treated only summarily in the very last lecture."[3]

Indeed, we are forced to consider *The Life of the Mind*, without Judging, as a tale without an ending. For we arrive at the end of the volume on *Willing* in something like a state of suspense. Willing, we are told, drives us into a theoretical impasse. Willing, if it means anything, implies an "abyss of pure spontaneity." But the established traditions of Occidental philosophy shied away from this abyss, sought to explain away the new by understanding it within the terms of the old. Only in Marxian utopianism was freedom in this sense of the genuinely new not abandoned. Arendt calls this a frustrating conclusion and says that she knows "of only one tentative alternative to it in our entire history of political thought": Augustine's notion of "natality," the human capacity for beginning, rooted in the fact of human birth. But on the last page of *Willing* we read that even the Augustinian theory "is somehow opaque":

> it seems to tell us no more than that we are *doomed* to be free by virtue of being born, no matter whether we like freedom or abhor its arbitrariness, are "pleased" with it or prefer to escape its awesome responsibility by electing some form of fatalism. This impasse, if such it is, cannot be opened or solved except by an appeal to another mental faculty, no less mysterious than the faculty of beginning, the faculty of Judgment, an analysis of which at least may tell us what is involved in our pleasures and displeasures.[4]

So we arrive at the threshold of Judging still in search of solutions to the basic problems that impelled Arendt to write *The Life of the Mind*. In this situation, it seems virtually an obligation to attempt to reconstruct her theory of judging, on the basis of lecture notes and posthumous material available to us, so that we can conjecture how she might have prepared her escape from the impasse in which she found herself at the end of the published text of *The Life of the Mind*.

It may seem highly speculative (not to say presumptuous) to endeavor to reconstruct what would have been contained in Judging had Arendt lived to complete this final chapter in her life's work. After all, we know that all she had completed at the time of her death was a single sheet, "blank except for the heading 'Judging' and two epigraphs." And the two epigraphs, interesting as they are, can hardly be said to offer a transparent guide to Arendt's intentions. The pathos of that single page seems almost to warn against proceeding. To complicate matters further, Arendt, in taking Kant as her guide to the faculty of judgment, tells us that she is addressing herself to a set of ideas that *he* never lived to develop properly.[5] So we are in the same position regarding Arendt as she herself was in relation to Kant. The task is doubly elusive. Still, there are persuasive reasons for thinking that the Kant lectures presented in this volume are a tolerably reliable indication of the work that was planned. For one thing, the account of judging in these lectures is entirely consistent with the passages on judging contained in the work that has been published, *Thinking*.[6] In fact, some passages from the latter work are taken, more or less verbatim, from the then-unpublished Kant lectures, which must indicate that she was reasonably satisfied with the understanding of judgment she had already formulated in them. Even more decisive is the fact that the outline of the theory of judgment she offered in a postscript to the *Thinking* volume corresponds very closely to the actual development of the Kant lectures (as we shall argue below). There is thus a foundation for assuming that the lectures on Kant's political philosophy offer a reasonable basis for re-constructing Hannah Arendt's theory of judging.

As if our undertaking were not already hazardous enough, there is a further difficulty to be contended with. Surveying Arendt's work as a whole, we can see that she offers not one but two theories of judgment. There are scattered references to the faculty of judgment throughout Arendt's published writings of the 1960s. However, beginning in 1970 we can detect a subtle but important reorientation. In her writings up until the 1971 essay, "Thinking and Moral Considerations,"[7] judgment is considered from the point of view of the *vita activa;* in her writings from that essay onward, judgment is considered from the point of view of the life of the mind. The emphasis shifts from the representative thought and enlarged mentality of political agents to the spectatorship and retrospective judgment of historians and storytellers. The blind poet, at a remove from the action and therefore capable of disinterested reflection, now becomes the emblem of judging.[8] Removed from first-order perception, the objects of judgment are re-presented in imagination by a mental act of second-order reflection. The blind poet judges from a distance, which is the condition of disinterestedness. Thus Homer prepares the way for the impartial judgments of ancient historiography. Homer and Herodotus alike proffer examples of human excellence for pleasurable reflection.[9]

As I interpret Arendt, her writings on the theme of judgment fall into two more or less distinct phases: early and late, practical and contemplative. I am aware that there are certain problems involved in dividing her works into "early" and "late." It would be unreasonable to expect any neat division into distinct periods, and to single out a particular date as marking a clear break between "early" and "late" will obviously appear in some respects arbitrary; one should not be surprised to encounter an overlap, both conceptual and chronological, between the two "phases." The point of the division, however, is to draw attention to the fact that in, say, the discussion of "representative thinking" in "Truth and Politics" there is as yet no concern with judging as a distinct mental activity (namely, as one of three articulations of mental life); here Arendt is concerned only with judging as a feature of political life. (In fact, it was only at a relatively late stage in her thinking that she came to see judging as an autonomous mental activity, distinct from thinking and willing.)[10] In what I call her "later" formulations, she is no longer concerned with judging as a feature of political life as such. What emerges instead is a conception of judging as one distinct articulation of the integral whole comprising the life of the mind. In order to challenge the conclusion that Arendt offers *two* distinct conceptions of judgment (the first relating to the world of praxis, the second to that of contemplation), one would need to give an account of precisely why, in her last writings, judging as an activity is placed exclusively within the life of the mind instead of being assigned a more equivocal status. The only explanation I myself can conceive of is that judgment had become for her a part of a concern very different from the original one, which had been a concern with the *vita activa,* the life of politics. The more she reflected on the faculty of judgment, the more inclined she was to regard it as the prerogative of the solitary (though public-spirited) contemplator as opposed to the actor (whose activity is necessarily nonsolitary). One acts with others; one judges by oneself (even though one does so by making present in one's imagination those who are absent). In judging, as understood by Arendt, one weighs the *possible* judgments of an imagined Other, not the actual judgments of real interlocutors.

In her earlier writings (for example, in "Freedom and Politics," "The Crisis in Culture," and "Truth and Politics")[11] Arendt had introduced the notion of judgment to give further grounding to her conception of political action as a plurality of actors acting in concert in a public space. Human beings can act as political beings because they can enter into the potential standpoints of others; they can share the world with others through judging what is held in common, and the objects of their judgments as political beings are the words and deeds that illuminate the space of appearances. In the later formulation, which begins to emerge in the Kant Lectures as well as in both "Thinking and Moral Considerations" and the *Thinking* volume, she approaches judging from a quite different, and much more ambitious, point of view. Here judgment is described as the "opening" or "solution" of an "impasse." Looking at the final chapter of *Willing*, we are able to reconstruct the nature of this impasse. The guiding concern of this last chapter, titled "The Abyss of Freedom and the *novus ordo seclorum*," is the problem of human freedom and its relationship to the faculty of willing. The implication is that only by analyzing the faculty that corresponds to "our pleasures and displeasures" can we find a way of embracing human freedom and of seeing it as bearable for natal and mortal beings like ourselves.

The Kant Lectures form an organic whole. The themes that inform them are all of a piece: the question of what gives meaning or worth to human life; the evaluation of life from the point of view of pleasure and displeasure; the hostility of the contemplative men to the world of human affairs; the unavailability of metaphysical truths and the need for critical thinking; the defense of common sense and of the common understanding of men; the dignity of man; the nature of historical reflection; the tension between Progress and the autonomy of the individual; the relationship between the universal and the particular; and, finally, the redemptive possibilities of human judgment. Despite the status of this material as mere notes for lectures, these themes are woven into a highly original meditation on whether man's worldly existence occasions gratitude for the givenness of being or whether, on the contrary, it is more likely to invite unrelieved melancholy.

According to Mary McCarthy, Arendt expected Judging to be much shorter than *Thinking* and *Willing* and to be the easiest to handle, but "one can guess that Judging might have surprised

her" and led her in unexpected directions.¹² This may well be so.
Still, one can discern a unity and consistency in the conception of
judgment that emerges from Arendt's discussions of this topic in
"Thinking and Moral Considerations" (1971), in volume 1 of *The
Life of the Mind,* and in the lecture notes published here. Furthermore, these writings, taken together, disclose an account of
judging that differs markedly from that to be found in her
writings prior to "Thinking and Moral Considerations." In
order to pinpoint what it is that gives Arendt's later theory its
coherence and sets it apart from the earlier account, it is necessary to trace the development of her thinking about the nature
of judgment. Let us, then, retrace the steps along which the idea
of judging developed in Arendt's work in order to see how a
concern with an interesting but long-neglected capacity of political man evolved into something far more ambitious—something
that promised affirmation of worldly affairs and the salvaging of
human freedom.

2. *Understanding and Historical Judgment*

THE THEMES AND CONCERNS that Arendt eventually wove into
the reflections on judging first emerged in her essay "Understanding and Politics," published in *Partisan Review* in 1953.¹³
Understanding "is an unending activity by which . . . we come to
terms with, reconcile ourselves to reality, that is, try to be at
home in the world" (p. 377). However, the activity of reconciliation becomes radically problematical in the century of totalitarianism, that is to say, in the wake of deeds to which we
seem incapable of being reconciled: "To the extent that the rise
of totalitarian governments is the central event of our world, to
understand totalitarianism is not to condone anything, but to
reconcile ourselves to a world in which these things are possible
at all" (ibid.).

"The result of understanding is meaning, which we originate
in the very process of living insofar as we try to reconcile ourselves to what we do and what we suffer" (p. 378). But, confronted by the unique horror of totalitarianism, we suddenly
discover "the fact that we have lost our tools of understanding.
Our quest for meaning is at the same time prompted and frustrated by our inability to originate meaning" (p. 383). Understanding is an activity that can be neither avoided nor concluded.

But we find ourselves faced with what seems like an insuperable problem, namely, that thinkers and political analysts, obliged to reflect on the historical fact of totalitarianism, are confronted by a phenomenon that appears to *resist* comprehension. The unprecedented evils of totalitarianism "have clearly exploded our categories of political thought and our standards for moral judgment" (p. 379). The task of understanding assumes proportions never before encountered in historical judgment.

The crisis in understanding is identical to a crisis in judgment, for understanding is "so closely related to and interrelated with judging that one must describe both as the subsumption" of something particular under a universal rule (p. 383). The trouble is that we no longer possess the reliable universal rules required for this subsumption; the inherited wisdom of the past fails us "as soon as we try to apply it honestly to the central political experiences of our own time" (p. 379). Even "normal" common-sense judgment no longer suffices: "we are living in a topsy-turvy world, a world where we cannot find our way by abiding by the rules of what once was common sense" (p. 383). According to Arendt, the growth of meaninglessness in the twentieth century has been accompanied by an atrophy of common sense, the faculty we ordinarily rely on to get our bearings in the world.

This moral and intellectual crisis of the West did not, however, originate with totalitarianism; it had its roots deep within the Western tradition. The demonic politics of the twentieth century merely exposed the latent crisis for all to see. Thus, what is frightening about the rise of totalitarianism is "that it has *brought to light* the ruin of our categories of thought and standards of judgment" (p. 388; my italics). Arendt points out that as early as the eighteenth century it was already evident to Montesquieu that only customs, mores, "prevented a spectacular moral and spiritual breakdown of occidental culture" (p. 384). Given a political body "held together only by customs and traditions," it is hardly surprising that European civilization proved vulnerable to the sweeping transformation wrought by the Industrial Revolution: "the great change took place within a political framework whose foundations were no longer secure and therefore overtook a society which, although it was still able to understand and to judge, could no longer give an account of its categories of understanding and standards of judgment when they were seriously challenged" (p. 385). By the nineteenth century, "our great tradition" was running out of answers to "the 'moral' and political questions of our own time.... The very sources from which such answers should have sprung had dried up. The very framework within which understanding and judging could arise is gone" (pp. 385–86).

Seen from the perspective of the historian, the story is at an end; but viewed from the perspective of the actor, we have no choice but to make a new start. Here Arendt invokes the principle of beginning discovered by Augustine, "the one great thinker who lived in a period which in some respects resembled our own more than any other in recorded history, and who in any case wrote under the full impact of a catastrophic end, which perhaps resembles the end to which we have come" (p. 390). Like Augustine, we live and think in the shadow of great catastrophe, and therefore, like him, we must attend to man's capacity for beginning; for man is the being whose essence is beginning.

> In the light of these reflections, our endeavoring to understand something which has ruined our categories of thought and our standards of judgment appears less frightening. Even though we have lost yardsticks by which to measure, and rules under which to subsume the particular, a being whose essence is beginning may have enough of origin within himself to understand without preconceived categories and to judge without the set of customary rules which is morality. If the essence of all, and in particular of political, action is to make a new beginning, then understanding becomes the other side of action, namely that form of cognition, in distinction from many others, by which acting men (and not men who are engaged in contemplating some progressive or doomed course of history) eventually can come to terms with what irrevocably happened and be reconciled with what unavoidably exists. [P. 391]

In other words, it is precisely when yardsticks of judgment disappear that the faculty of judgment comes into its own.

Arendt ends the essay by relating understanding to the faculty of imagination, which she distinguishes from mere fancy:

> Imagination alone enables us to see things in their proper perspective, to put that which is too close at a certain distance so that we can see and understand it without bias and prejudice, to bridge abysses of remoteness until we can see and understand everything that is too far away from us as though

it were our own affair. This "distancing" of some things and bridging the abysses to others is part of the dialogue of understanding. [P. 392]

Imagination allows for the proximity that makes understanding possible, and it also establishes the distance needed for judgment.

Without this kind of imagination, which actually is understanding, we would never be able to take our bearings in the world. It is the only inner compass we have. . . . If we want to be at home on this earth, even at the price of being at home in this century, we must try to take part in the interminable dialogue with its essence. [Ibid.]

3. Judging Eichmann

ACCORDING TO Hannah Arendt, "thought itself arises out of incidents of living experience and must remain bound to them as the only guideposts by which to take its bearings."[14] If this is so, what particular experience gave rise to her theory of judging? Needless to say, her work on the rise of totalitarianism is relevant: it alerted her to the complexities of human judgment and to the threats posed to it by developments in modern society. But there is good reason for supposing that another, more specific, though obviously related "incident of living experience" precipitated her efforts to theorize about the nature of judgment, namely, her presence at the trial of Adolf Eichmann in Jerusalem in 1961. Her report of the trial, which appeared in 1963, first in the *New Yorker* and then in book form, generated a huge storm of controversy.[15] We know that this experience provided the impetus for wide-ranging reflection on her part, for she herself informs us that her reflections on the status of truth and on the critical function of thought were motivated by her involvement in the Eichmann controversy.[16] There is thus little reason to doubt that what was preoccupying her when she began to think seriously about judgment was the unavoidable need to render judgment in the case of Adolf Eichmann, together with the fact that Eichmann himself clearly abstained from responsible judgment—an evil generated by his "thought-defying" banality.

There are two main sources for assessing the impact the Eichmann trial had on Arendt's concept of judging: a lecture

"Personal Responsibility under Dictatorship," published in *The Listener* in 1964,[17] and a Postscript added to the second (1965) edition of *Eichmann in Jerusalem*. The question that lies at the heart of these two pieces is whether we are entitled to presuppose "an independent human faculty, unsupported by law and public opinion, that judges anew in full spontaneity every deed and intent whenever the occasion arises." Do we possess such a faculty, and are we lawgivers, every single one of us, whenever we act?[18] Arendt says that this "touches upon one of the central moral questions of all time, namely upon the nature and function of human judgment."[19] What had been demanded in both the Eichmann and Nuremberg trials was

> that human beings be capable of telling right from wrong even when all they have to guide them is their own judgment, which, moreover, happens to be completely at odds with what they must regard as the unanimous opinion of all those around them. . . . Those few who were still able to tell right from wrong went really only by their own judgments, and they did so freely; there were no rules to be abided by, under which the particular cases with which they were confronted could be subsumed. They had to decide each instance as it arose, because no rules existed for the unprecedented.[20]

There is a second aspect involved here, which is in some ways equally disturbing, for it too places in question the very status of judgment itself. In *Eichmann in Jerusalem* Arendt had sought to do justice to the Holocaust experience not by representing the war criminals as subhuman creatures, who are beneath judgment, or the victims as innocents without responsibility, who surpass judgment, but by making clear that human judgment can function only where those judged are neither beasts nor angels but men. However, many of Arendt's readers objected (quite vociferously) that if this is how human judgment must operate, it would be better to abstain from judgment altogether. Arendt notes that the uproar occasioned by the Eichmann book shows "how troubled men of our time are by this question of judgment."[21] This whole issue was confronted most directly in the fascinating exchange of letters in *Encounter* magazine between Gershom Scholem and Arendt.[22] Arendt's final reply is contained in the Postscript to the revised edition of *Eichmann in Jerusalem*, where she writes: "The argument that we cannot judge if we were not present and involved ourselves seems to convince everyone everywhere, although it seems obvious that *if it were true, neither the administration of justice nor the writing of history would ever be possible.*"[23] This point is unassailable. A second argument, that the person who judges cannot avoid the reproach of self-righteousness, proves upon examination to be no more valid than the first. Arendt responded to it by saying: "Even the judge who condemns a murderer can still say when he goes home: 'And there, but for the grace of God, go I.'" Moreover, "the reflection that you yourself might have done wrong under the same circumstances may kindle a spirit of forgiveness," but this in no way preempts judgment. For Arendt, forgiveness *follows* judgment, it does not displace it: "Justice, but not mercy, is a matter of judgment."[24]

Arendt states that public opinion everywhere seems to be in happy agreement that "no one has the right to judge somebody else. What public opinion permits us to judge and even to condemn are trends, or whole groups of people—the larger the better—in short, something so general that distinctions can no longer be made, names no longer named."[25] Thus we find, for instance, a flourishing of theories of the collective guilt or collective innocence of entire peoples. "All these clichés have in common that they make judgment superfluous and that to utter them is devoid of all risk."[26] This goes with a "reluctance evident everywhere to make judgments in terms of individual moral responsibility."[27] The sad irony is that this atrophy of the faculty of judgment was precisely what had made Eichmann's monstrous crimes possible in the first place.

The Eichmann affair brought to Arendt's full awareness judgment's function of assimilating in a humanly intelligible way whatever most strenuously resists such assimilation. Judgment brings its objects of judgment within the reach of human meaningfulness. This is brought to light most strikingly in the exchange between Arendt and Gershom Scholem over the Eichmann question. Scholem wrote in his letter to Arendt: "There were among [the elders of the Jews] many people in no way different from ourselves, who were compelled to make terrible decisions in circumstances that we cannot even begin to reproduce or reconstruct. I do not know whether they were right or wrong. *Nor do I presume to judge.* I was not there." Arendt replied: "[The behavior of Jewish functionaries] constitutes our part of the so-called 'unmastered past,' and although you may be right that it is too early for a 'balanced judgment' (though I doubt this), I do believe that *we shall only come to terms with this past if we begin to judge* and to be frank about it."[28] Thus judgment serves to help us make sense of, to render humanly intelligible, events that otherwise could not be made so. The faculty of judgment is in the service of human intelligibility—the very same service that Arendt ascribes to the telling of excellent deeds in a story—and conferring intelligibility is the meaning of politics.

In this respect, Arendt's *Eichmann in Jerusalem* bears comparison with another work of similar moral dimensions, Maurice Merleau-Ponty's *Humanism and Terror*. These two books are addressed to the two most extreme (and most distressing) political experiences of our century, Naziism and Stalinism, respectively. What the two works share is that both place the effort to understand at the center of their respective inquiries. When understanding is placed in the service of judgment, it requires the free exercise of imagination—in particular, the ability to imagine how things look from a position that we do not in fact occupy. Judgment may require us to make the effort to understand those whose point of view we not only do not share but may even find highly distasteful. Disagreement does not release us from the responsibility to understand what we reject; if anything, it rather heightens this responsibility. Merleau-Ponty writes: "true liberty takes others as they are, tries to understand even those doctrines which are its negation, *and never allows itself to judge before understanding.* We must fulfill our freedom of thought in the freedom of understanding."[29] For Merleau-Ponty too, judgment assumes the tragic tasks of understanding and forgiving, these composing the tragic dimensions of judgment. Arendt's efforts to come to terms with the experience of the Holocaust convey the same message. To judge a genuinely human situation is to partake of the tragedy that is potential in circumstances where human responsibility is exercised and borne to its limit. This helps to explain why Arendt associates the faculty of judging with the sense of human dignity.

The relevance of the Eichmann case for the theme of judging is twofold: first, there is the inability of Eichmann himself to think and to judge—to tell right from wrong, beautiful from ugly—in the critical political situation in which he was involved; second, there is the problem of retrospective understanding, of how to judge the meaning of Eichmann from a vantage point temporally and spatially removed from the events in question.

Arendt is concerned with both dimensions of this twofold relevance: the first, in which Eichmann is the judging subject; the second, in which Arendt herself and her fellow American Jews are called upon to judge. The lesson of the first is that inability to think has fatal implications for the faculty of judging. The lesson of the second is that the responsibility for making judgments cannot be shirked even when commitments and allegiances of a familial or national kind would seem to intrude. The activity of judging cannot be inhibited by supposedly prior relations of love or loyalty. Judgment must be free, and the condition of its autonomy is the ability to think.

The second of these two dimensions of the Eichmann case—namely, the retrospective judgment of the Jewish-American community two decades later—poses, as we have seen, a challenge to the very status of judgment. For the issue is whether one ought perhaps, out of concern or the fear of committing a betrayal, to suspend judgment altogether. Arendt's reply is uncompromising and unconditional. Without judgments by which to render our world intelligible, the space of appearances would simply collapse. The right of judgment is therefore absolute and inalienable, for it is by constantly pronouncing judgments that we are able to make sense of the world to ourselves. If we forfeited our faculty of judgment, through love or diffidence, we would be sure to lose our bearings in the world.

4. Taste and Culture

It is in an article by Arendt entitled "Freedom and Politics," published in 1961, that we first encounter the idea that Kant's *Critique of Judgment* contains the seeds of a political philosophy distinct from, and indeed opposed to, the political philosophy associated with the *Critique of Practical Reason*. Arendt writes that Kant

> expounds two political philosophies which differ sharply from one another—the first being that which is generally accepted as such in his *Critique of Practical Reason* and the second that contained in his *Critique of Judgment*. That the first part of the latter is, in reality, a political philosophy is a fact that is seldom mentioned in works on Kant; on the other hand, it can, I think, be seen from all his political writings that for Kant himself the theme of "judgment" carries more weight

than that of "practical reason." In the *Critique of Judgment* freedom is portrayed as a predicate of the power of imagination and not of the will, and the power of imagination is linked most closely with that wider manner of thinking which is political thinking par excellence, because it enables us to "put ourselves in the minds of other men."[30]

The theory of judging delineated in Arendt's subsequently published works consists simply in the endeavor to draw out and develop this "other" (hitherto unknown or unappreciated) political philosophy.

Among the writings published in her lifetime, Arendt's fullest account of judgment is contained in her essay "The Crisis in Culture: Its Social and Its Political Significance," included in *Between Past and Future*.[31] The basis of Arendt's analysis in "The Crisis in Culture" is a triadic differentiation between things (cultural objects), values (exchange values), and consumer goods. The rightful dignity of cultural goods inheres in their being "things," that is, "permanent appurtenances of the world" whose "excellence is measured by their ability to withstand the life process" (pp. 205–6). These cultural objects were degraded into "values" by the cultural philistinism of eighteenth- and nineteenth-century "good society," since they were used as exchange values for social advancement by the educated European bourgeoisie. The subsequent rise of mass society has brought a new development: the abandonment of culture as an exchange value and the substitution for it of a concern with something of a wholly different nature: entertainment. (Mass man is defined by "his capacity for consumption, accompanied by inability to judge, or even to distinguish," as well as a "fateful alienation from the world") (p. 199). Entertainment is a "consumer good" in the strict sense, an integral part of man's "metabolism with nature," "consumed" as soon as it serves the need for which it was intended, along with everything else produced-and-consumed in a laboring society (the distinction between exchange values and consumer goods obviously corresponds to Arendt's distinction between work and labor in *The Human Condition*). The consumerism of a laboring society, Arendt believes, is in a sense a lesser threat to culture than was the philistinism of "good society" because its preoccupation with entertainment has nothing whatever to do with culture and therefore does not infringe upon it the way philistinism did. On the other hand, culture, too, is eventually absorbed into the consumer society's need for entertainment, by virtue of an all-encompassing functionalization:

> Culture relates to objects and is a phenomenon of the world; entertainment relates to people and is a phenomenon of life. An object is cultural to the extent that it can endure; its durability is the very opposite of functionality, which is the quality which makes it disappear again from the phenomenal world by being used and used up. The great user and consumer of objects is life itself, the life of the individual and the life of society as a whole. Life is indifferent to the thingness of an object; it insists that every thing must be functional, fulfill some needs. Culture is being threatened when all worldly objects and things, produced by the present or the past, are treated as mere functions for the life process of society, as though they are there only to fulfill some need. [P. 208]

> [A] consumers' society cannot possibly know how to take care of a world and the things which belong exclusively to the space of worldly appearances, because its central attitude toward all objects, the attitude of consumption, spells ruin to everything it touches. [P. 211]

What this tells us is that the cultural and the political both involve caring for the world, that both converge upon concern for the public world. Politics and culture are not essentially separate spheres of human endeavor: both are concerned with how the world looks, how it appears to those who share it, and both attend to the quality of the worldly dwelling that envelops us and in which we pass our mortal existence.

This is brought out very well in a striking passage from Pericles' Funeral Oration, as rendered by Thucydides, which Arendt translates as: "We love beauty within the limits of political judgment, and we philosophize without the barbarian vice of effeminacy" (p. 214). The reason "love of beauty" can be encompassed within "political judgment" is that they share the fundamental requirement of public appearance, they presuppose a common world. "The common element connecting art and politics is that they both are phenomena of the public world":

> [C]ulture indicates that the public realm, which is rendered politically secure by men of action, offers its space of display to those things whose essence it is to appear and to be beautiful. In others words, culture indicates that art and politics, their conflicts and tensions notwithstanding, are interrelated

and even mutually dependent. Seen against the background of political experiences and of activities which, if left to themselves, come and go without leaving any trace in the world, beauty is the very manifestation of imperishability. The fleeting greatness of word and deed can endure in the world to the extent that beauty is bestowed upon it. Without the beauty, that is, the radiant glory in which potential immortality is made manifest in the human world, all human life would be futile and no greatness could endure. [P. 218]

Taste, the discriminating, discerning, judging activity of love of beauty, is the *cultura animi,* the possession of "a mind so trained and cultivated that it can be trusted to tend and take care of a world of appearances whose criterion is beauty" (p. 219).

Arendt introduces her discussion of judgment in connection with "the spectator" who apprehends cultural and political appearances. Kant's *Critique of Judgment* is now appealed to, she tells us, because in the first part, the "Critique of Aesthetic Judgment," it offers "an analytic of the beautiful primarily from the viewpoint of the judging spectator" (pp. 219–20). This concern with the judging spectator is simply the extension of Arendt's definition of politics in terms of virtuosity or performance (p. 153). The deeds of the actor are as in need of the spectator's judgment as those of any other performer. Arendt begins her account of this idea of spectatorship by calling attention to the plurality presupposed in judgment as opposed to the solitary nature of thought. She refers to the Kantian notion of "enlarged mentality," which she elsewhere speaks of as "representative thinking": "thinking in the place of everybody else" (p. 241). This involves "potential agreement with others," coming finally to some agreement.

A further aspect of judgment is that, unlike logical reasoning, it does not compel universal validity. Rather, it appeals to judging persons who are "present," who are members of the public realm where the objects of judgment appear. Arendt appeals to the Aristotelian distinction between *phronēsis* and *sophia:* the latter strives to rise above common sense; the former is rooted in common sense, which "discloses to us the nature of the world insofar as it is a common world"; it "enables man to orient himself in the public realm, in the common world." This defense of common sense, it should be noted, is a persistent theme in Arendt's work. Common sense means sharing a nonsubjective and "objective" (object-laden) world with others. "Judging is one, if not the most, important activity in which this sharing-the-world-with-others comes to pass" (p. 221).

Arendt credits Kant with having dislodged the prejudice that judgments of taste, concerning merely aesthetic matters, lie therefore outside the political realm (as well as outside the domain of reason). She claims that the alleged subjective arbitrariness of taste offended not Kant's aesthetic but his political sense. It is because of his awareness of the public quality of beauty and the public relevance of beautiful things, she maintains, that Kant insisted that judgments of taste are open to discussion and subject to dispute.

> In aesthetic no less than in political judgments, a decision is made, and although this decision is always determined by a certain subjectivity, by the simple fact that each person occupies a place of his own from which he looks upon and judges the world, it also derives from the fact that the world itself is an objective datum, something common to all its inhabitants. The activity of taste decides how this world, independent of its utility and our vital interests in it, is to look and sound, what men will see and what they will hear in it. Taste judges the world in its appearance and in its worldliness; its interest in the world is purely "disinterested," and that means that neither the life interests of the individual nor the moral interests of the self are involved here. For judgments of taste, the world is the primary thing, not man, neither man's life nor his self. [P. 222]

Arendt returns to the contrast between judgment and philosophical argument oriented toward truth. The latter, demonstrable truth, seeks to *compel* agreement by a process of compelling proof. Judgments of taste, by contrast, are, like political opinions, persuasive; they are characterized by "the hope of *coming* to an agreement with everyone else eventually."

> Culture and politics . . . belong together because it is not knowledge or truth which is at stake, but rather judgment and decision, the judicious exchange of opinion about the sphere of public life and the common world, and the decision what manner of action is to be taken in it, as well as to how it is to look henceforth, what kinds of things are to appear in it. [P. 223]

Arendt concludes her discussion of taste in "The Crisis in Culture" with an affirmation of humanism, with specific reference to Cicero. Taste, she points out, "decides not only how the world is to look, but also who belongs together in it." It defines a principle of belonging, is an expression of the company one keeps, and, as such, like politics itself, it is a matter of self-disclosure.[32] Thus "taste is the political capacity that truly humanizes the beautiful and creates a culture" (p. 224). Arendt interprets Cicero to be saying that "for the true humanist neither the verities of the scientist nor the truth of the philosopher nor the beauty of the artist can be absolutes; the humanist, because he is not a specialist, exerts a faculty of judgment and taste which is beyond the coercion which each specialty imposes upon us" (p. 225). Against specialization and philistinism, Arendt counter-poses a humanism that "knows how to take care and preserve and admire the things of the world" (ibid.). She concludes from these reflections upon taste that a cultivated person ought to be "one who knows how to choose his company among men, among things, among thoughts, in the present as well as in the past" (p. 226).[33]

5. *Representative Thinking*

THE ALL-IMPORTANT CONTRAST between persuasive judgment and compelling truth is further developed in Arendt's essay "Truth and Politics."[34] Here she places it in the context of the traditional conflict between the philosophical life and the life of the citizen. The philosophers opposed to truth "mere opinion, which was equated with illusion, and it was this degrading of opinion that gave the conflict its political poignancy; for opinion, and not truth, belongs among the indispensable prerequisites of all power." This antagonism between truth and opinion is such that

> every claim in the sphere of human affairs to an absolute truth, whose validity needs no support from the side of opinion, strikes at the very roots of all politics and all governments. [P. 233]

Arendt appeals to Madison, Lessing, and Kant in trying to resist the aspersions cast on opinion by philosophers, from Plato onward, and the devaluation of the life of the citizen that these imply. Opinion derives its own distinctive dignity from the condition of human plurality, from the need for the citizen to address himself to his fellows; for "debate constitutes the very essence of political life." The trouble, as Arendt sees it, is that all truth, by peremptorily claiming to be acknowledged, precludes debate: "The modes of thought and communication that deal with truth, if seen from the political perspective, are necessarily domineering; they do not take into account other people's opinions, and taking these into account is the hallmark of all strictly political thinking" (p. 241).

It is here that Arendt introduces her notion of the representative character of political thought:

> I form an opinion by considering a given issue from different viewpoints, by making present to my mind the standpoints of those who are absent; that is, I represent them. This process of representation does not blindly adopt the actual views of those who stand somewhere else, and hence look upon the world from a different perspective; this is a question neither of empathy, as though I tried to be or to feel like somebody else, nor of counting noses and joining a majority but of being and thinking in my own identity where actually I am not. The more people's standpoints I have present in my mind while I am pondering a given issue, and the better I can imagine how I would feel and think if I were in their place, the stronger will be my capacity for representative thinking and the more valid my final conclusions, my opinion. [Ibid.]

This capacity, according to Arendt, is the Kantian "enlarged mentality," which is the basis for man's ability to judge (though Kant, having discovered this capacity for impartial judgment, "did not recognize the political and moral implications of his discovery" [ibid.]). We try to *imagine* what it would be like to be somewhere else in thought, and "the only condition for this exertion of the imagination is disinterestedness, the liberation from one's own private interests" (p. 242). This process of opinion formation, determined by those in whose place somebody thinks and uses his own mind, is such that "a particular issue is forced into the open that it may show itself from all sides, in every possible perspective, until it is flooded and made transparent by the full light of human comprehension" (ibid.).

Arendt illustrates this notion of representative thinking in an unpublished lecture on judgment:

> Suppose I look at a specific slum dwelling and I perceive in this particular building the general notion which it does not exhibit directly, the notion of poverty and misery. I arrive at this notion by representing to myself how I would feel if I had

to live there, that is, I try to think in the place of the slum-dweller. The judgment I shall come up with will by no means necessarily be the same as that of the inhabitants, whom time and hopelessness may have dulled to the outrage of their condition, but it will become for my further judging of these matters an outstanding example to which I refer.... Furthermore, while I take into account others when judging, this does not mean that I conform in my judgment to those of others, I still speak with my own voice and I do not count noses in order to arrive at what I think is right. But my judgment is no longer subjective either.[35]

"The point of the matter," says Arendt, "is that my judgment of a particular instance does not merely depend upon my perception, but upon my representing to myself something which I do not perceive."[36]

It is clear that judgment and opinion belong inextricably together as the chief faculties of political reason. Arendt's intention is fairly obvious: to concentrate attention on the faculty of judgment is to rescue opinion from the disrepute into which it has fallen since Plato. Both faculties, that of judging and that of forming opinions, are thus redeemed simultaneously. This is brought out very well in a passage from *On Revolution,* where judgment and opinion are spoken of in the same breath: "opinion and judgment, ... these two politically most important, rational faculties, had been almost entirely neglected by the tradition of political as well as philosophic thought."[37] She notes that the Founding Fathers of the American Revolution were made aware of the importance of these two faculties, in spite of the fact that they "did not try consciously to reassert the rank and dignity of opinion in the hierarchy of human rational abilities. The same is true with respect to judgment, where we would have to turn to Kant's philosophy, rather than to the men of the revolutions, if we wished to learn something about its essential character and amazing range in the realm of human affairs."[38] The Founding Fathers themselves were not able to transcend "the narrow and tradition-bound framework of their general concepts" to the extent of reconceptualizing these two rational faculties of political life. In other words, the required reassertion is still awaited, and to formulate it is a task that Arendt herself undertakes as expositor of Kant.

We can now see the real import of Arendt's opposition between philosophical truth and the judgment of the citizen. Her

aim is to bolster the "rank and dignity" of opinion. It is judgment
that gives to opinion its own distinctive dignity, lending it a measure of respectability when it is weighed against truth. It is on
account of judgment that opinion is not the disgrace that philosophers have traditionally made it out to be. It is because we, as
plural beings, can engage in "representative thinking" that
opinion cannot be as summarily dismissed as traditional philosophy assumed. And since opinion is the mainstay of politics, an
upgrading of the status of opinion serves at the same time to
elevate the status of the political.

Thus far, Arendt's theorizing about the nature of judgment
has followed a consistent line of development. However, when
we turn to her writings of the 1970s, we find in her reflections on
judging a discernible shift of emphasis. No longer does she stress
the representative thinking of political agents. Instead, judging
is aligned with thinking, which "has no political relevance unless
special emergencies arise."[39] Instead of being conceived in
terms of the deliberations of political actors deciding on possible
courses of future action (an activity Arendt subsequently
identifies with projects of the will), judging now comes to be
defined as reflection on the past, on what is already given, and,
in common with thinking, "such reflections will inevitably arise
in political emergencies."[40]

6. The Wind of Thought:
Judging in Emergencies

THE LATER SET OF CONCERNS, which Arendt subsequently
treated in *The Life of the Mind*, first emerged in print in "Thinking and Moral Considerations: A Lecture," an article published
in 1971.[41] At the end of the essay Arendt turns to the role of the
faculty of judgment. In times of historical crisis, she writes,
"thinking ceases to be a marginal affair in political matters" because those who possess the capacity for critical thought are not
swept away unthinkingly, like everyone else:

> their refusal to join is conspicuous and thereby becomes a
> kind of action. The purging element in thinking, Socrates'
> midwifery, that brings out the implications of unexamined
> opinions and thereby destroys them—values, doctrines,
> theories, and even convictions—is political by implication. For

this destruction has a liberating effect on another human faculty, the faculty of judgment, which one may call, with some justification, the most political of man's mental abilities. It is the faculty to judge *particulars* without subsuming them under those general rules which can be taught and learned until they grow into habits that can be replaced by other habits and rules.

The faculty of judging particulars (as Kant discovered it), the ability to say, "this is wrong," "this is beautiful," etc., is not the same as the faculty of thinking. Thinking deals with invisibles, with representations of things that are absent; judging always concerns particulars and things close at hand. But the two are interrelated in a way similar to the way consciousness and conscience are interconnected. If thinking, the two-in-one of the soundless dialogue, actualizes the difference within our identity as given in consciousness and thereby results in conscience as its by-product, then judging, the by-product of the liberating effect of thinking, realizes thinking, makes it manifest in the world of appearances, where I am never alone and always much too busy to be able to think. The manifestation of the wind of thought is no knowledge; it is the ability to tell right from wrong, beautiful from ugly. And this indeed may prevent catastrophes, at least for myself, in the rare moments when the chips are down.[42]

For Arendt, politics is defined by phenomenality, as self-disclosure in a space of appearances. Political things, as Arendt conceives them, are phenomenally manifest: "great things are self-evident, shine by themselves," the poet or historiographer merely *preserving* the glory that is already visible to all. Among the Greeks, "great deeds and great words were, in their greatness, as real as a stone or a house, there to be seen and heard by everybody present. Greatness was easily recognizable."[43] Again, it is this that connects art and politics: "both are phenomena of the public world."[44] The phenomenality of politics is therefore analogous to the phenomenality of art:

in order to become aware of appearances we first must be free to establish a certain distance between ourselves and the object, and the more important the sheer appearance of a thing is, the more distance it requires for its proper appreciation. This distance cannot arise unless we are in a position to forget ourselves, the cares and interests and urges of our lives, so that we will not seize what we admire but let it be as it is, in its appearance.[45]

This point is expressed very well by Ernst Vollrath in an excellent article on Hannah Arendt's "method of political thinking." Vollrath writes that impartiality (as distinct from objectivity)

> implies essentially "to say what is," . . . to recognize phenomena in their facticity and to determine this facticity in a phenomenal sense rather than to construe it from an epistemic basis. . . . Hannah Arendt's kind of political thinking regards topics within the political field not as "objects" but as phenomena and appearances. They are what shows itself, what appears to the eyes and senses. . . . Political events are phenomena in a special sense; one might say that they are phenomena *per se.* . . . The space in which political phenomena occur is created by the phenomena themselves.[46]

Judgment discriminates among the self-disclosive phenomena and captures phenomenal appearance in its fullness. Accordingly, the capacity of judgment for discerning the qualities of the particular without prior subsumption under a universal is closely related to the nature of politics as disclosure. Judgment, as it were, confirms the being of that which has been disclosed. Thus it is in a very emphatic sense that human judgment always proceeds in a world of appearances.

The objects of our judgment are particulars that open themselves to our purview. Naturally, we can apprehend particulars only to the extent that we class them under some universal. A bare (unclassed) particular is not a possible object of judgment. But when the universals under which we subsume those judged particulars turn into fixed habits of thought, ossified rules and standards, "conventional, standardized codes of expression and conduct,"[47] the danger is that we will not open ourselves fully to the phenomenal richness of the appearances that make themselves available for our judgment. It is in this situation that the faculty of judgment undergoes its most severe test, and the acuteness or dullness of our judgments will have real practical consequences. For instance, for those accustomed to the ordinary brutality and oppression of conventional tyrannies, despotisms, and dictatorships, it was difficult to recognize in twentieth-century totalitarianism something entirely novel and unprecedented.[48] It requires a special quality of judgment to discriminate between what we are used to and what is genuinely new and different. Those who possess taste, who are discriminating in things beautiful and ugly, good and bad, will be less likely to be caught off their guard in times of political crisis.

According to Arendt, thought—the critical movement of thinking—loosens the hold of universals (e.g., entrenched moral habits ossified into inflexible general precepts) and thus frees judgment to operate in an open space of moral or aesthetic discrimination and discernment. Judgment functions best when this space has been cleared for it by critical thinking. In this way, the universal does not domineer over the particular; rather, the latter can be apprehended as it truly discloses itself. Thinking itself thereby assumes a political relevance by virtue of its relationship to the faculty of judgment. By loosening the grip of the universal over the particular, thinking releases the political potency of the faculty of judgment—the potency that inheres in its capacity to perceive things as they are, that is, as they are phenomenally manifest.[49]

In her lectures on "Basic Moral Propositions," given in Chicago in 1966, and, before that, in a lecture course, "Some Questions of Moral Philosophy," given at the New School for Social Research in 1965, Arendt had described how Western morality has been rendered so vulnerable by developments in Western politics that what formerly were regarded as basic ethical tenets of Western civilization ("It is better to suffer wrong than to do wrong," "Do unto others as you would have them do unto you," etc.) have come to be devalued to the level of mere conventions (as easily exchangeable as a set of table manners).[50] It is in this context that Arendt turns to Kant, seeking an account of moral life that recognizes the nonself-evidency of moral propositions yet does not require that we forgo moral judgment altogether. Kant's analysis of taste provides the concepts of communication, intersubjective agreement, and shared judgment that Arendt seeks for the reconstruction of moral horizons. If we can no longer count on the presumption of moral objectivity, perhaps we can at least hope to find a way out of pure subjectivity by appealing to a notion of moral taste that can act as a bridge between judging subjects brought into a company of shared or agreed judgments. At the same time, Arendt sought an account of evil that would allow her to come to grips with the political evils of the twentieth century. Here again the analysis of judgment is central, for it is here that she locates the source of the greatest evils in the political realm, the evil of totalitarianism epitomized in Eichmann: "In the refusal to judge: lack of imagination, of having present before your eyes and taking into account the others whom you must represent."[51]

This evil implicit in the refusal to judge is addressed at the end of the final lecture of the course on "Basic Moral Propositions":

> In the last analysis . . . our decisions about right and wrong will depend upon our choice of company, with whom we wish to spend our lives. And this company [in turn] is chosen through thinking in examples, in examples of persons dead or alive, and in examples of incidents, past or present. In the unlikely case that someone should come and tell us that he would prefer Bluebeard for company, and hence as his example, all we could do would be to make sure that he would never come near us. But the likelihood that someone would come and tell us that he does not mind and that any company will be good enough for him is, I fear, by far greater. Morally and even politically speaking, this indifference, though common enough, is the greatest danger. And in the same direction, only a bit less dangerous, does this other very common modern phenomenon lie, the widespread tendency to refuse to judge at all. Out of the unwillingness or inability to choose one's examples and one's company, and out of the unwillingness or inability to relate to others through judgment, arise the real *skandala*, the real stumbling-blocks which human powers cannot remove because they were not caused by human and humanly understandable motives. Therein lies the horror and, at the same time, the banality of evil.[52]

The real danger in contemporary societies is that the bureaucratic, technocratic, and depoliticized structures of modern life encourage indifference and increasingly render men less discriminating, less capable of critical thinking, and less inclined to assume responsibility.[53]

Arendt's theory of judging is thus placed within an overall account of the present historical situation, which she interprets as one of a general crisis of Western morals and politics: traditional standards of judgment are no longer authoritative,[54] ultimate values have ceased to be binding, the norms of political and moral civility have become acutely vulnerable. In this situation, the best that we can hope for is "agreement in judgments" within an ideal judging community. The supreme danger is abstention from judgment, the banality of evil, the danger that, "when the chips are down," the self will surrender to the forces of evil rather than exercise autonomous judgment. As long as we continue to discriminate among things good and beautiful, as long as we continue to "choose our company" in matters of taste and politics—that is, as long as we refuse to forgo our faculty of judgment—all is not lost.

These same issues are raised in a very interesting way in an exchange between Arendt and Hans Jonas that occurred at a conference on "The Work of Hannah Arendt" held at York University in November, 1972, the transcript of which has recently been published in a volume edited by Melvyn Hill, *Hannah Arendt: The Recovery of the Public World.*[55]

JONAS: That there is at the bottom of all our being and of our action the desire to share the world with other men is incontestable, but we want to share a certain world with certain men. And if it is the task of politics to make the world a fitting home for man, that raises the question: "What is a fitting home for man?"

It can only be decided if we form some idea of what man is or ought to be. And that again cannot be determined, except arbitrarily, if we cannot make appeal to some truth about man which can validate judgment of this kind, and the derivative judgment of political taste that crops up in the concrete situations—and especially if it is a question of deciding how the future world should look—which we have to do all the time dealing with technological enterprises that are having an impact on the total dispensation of things.

Now it is not the case that Kant simply made appeal to judgment. He also made appeal to the concept of the good. There is such an idea as the supreme good however we define it. And perhaps it escapes definition. It cannot be an entirely empty concept and it is related to our conception of what man is. In other words, that which has by unanimous consensus here been declared dead and done with—namely, metaphysics—has to be called in at some place to give us a final directive.

Our powers of decision reach far beyond the handling of immediate situations and of the short-term future. Our powers of doing or acting now extend over such matters as really involve a judgment or an insight into or a faith in—I leave that open—some ultimates. For in ordinary politics as it has been understood until the twentieth century we could do with penultimates. It is not true that the condition of the commonwealth had to be decided by the really ultimate values or standards. When it is a matter, as it is under the conditions of modern technology, that willy-nilly we are embarking on courses which affect the total condition of things on earth and

the total future condition of man, then I don't think we can
simply wash our hands and say Western metaphysics has got
us into an impasse and we declare it bankrupt and we appeal
now to shareable judgments—where, for God's sake, we do
not mean by shared judgments shared with a majority or
shared with any defined group. We can share judgments to
our perdition with many, but we must make an appeal beyond
that sphere!

Arendt does not really face up to this question of the ultimate
cognitive status of shared judgments; instead, she deflects the
argument to historical and sociological considerations.

ARENDT: . . . Now if our future should depend on what you
say now—namely, that we will get an ultimate which from
above will decide for us (and then the question is, of course,
who is going to recognize this ultimate and which will be the
rules for recognizing this ultimate—you have really an infinite
regress here, but anyhow) I would be utterly pessimistic. If
that is the case, then we are lost. Because this actually demands that a new god will appear. . . .

For instance, I am perfectly sure that this whole totalitarian
catastrophe would not have happened if people still had believed in God, or in hell rather—that is, if there still were
ultimates. There were no ultimates. And you know as well as I
do that there were no ultimates which one could with validity
appeal to. One couldn't appeal to anybody.

And if you go through such a situation [as totalitarianism],
the first thing you know is the following: you *never* know how
somebody will act. You have the surprise of your life! This
goes throughout all layers of society, and it goes throughout
various distinctions between men. And if you want to make a
generalization, then you could say that those who were still
very firmly convinced of the so-called old values were the first
to be ready to change their old values for a new set of values,
provided they were given one. And I am afraid of this, because I think that the moment you give anybody a new set of
values—or this famous "bannister"—you can immediately exchange it. [Arendt is referring here to "thinking without a
bannister," *Denken ohne Geländer,* a phrase she had coined
to convey the fact that we no longer possess a secure set of
ultimate values to guide our thought.—R. B.] And the only
thing the guy gets used to is having a "bannister" and a set of
values, no matter. I do not believe that we can stabilize the

situation in which we have been since the seventeenth century
in any final way. . . .
   We wouldn't have to bother about this whole business if
metaphysics and this whole value business hadn't fallen down.
We begin to question because of these events.

Rather than press his question, Jonas backtracks, claiming for
judgment—as Arendt does—only a negative or limiting check
upon practice:

> JONAS: I share with Hannah Arendt the position that we are
> not in possession of any ultimates, either by knowledge or by
> conviction or faith. And I also believe that we cannot have this
> as a command performance because "we need it so bitterly we
> therefore should have it."
>   However, a part of wisdom is knowledge of ignorance. The
> Socratic attitude is to know that one does not know. And this
> realization of our ignorance can be of great practical im-
> portance in the exercise of the power of judgment, which is
> after all related to action in the political sphere, into future
> action, and far-reaching action.
>   Our enterprises have an eschatological tendency in
> them—a built-in utopianism, namely, to move towards ulti-
> mate situations. Lacking the knowledge of ultimate
> values—or, of what is ultimately desirable—or, of what is man
> so that the world can be fitting for man, we should at least
> abstain from allowing eschatological situations to come about.
> This alone is a very important practical injunction that we can
> draw from the insight that only with some conception of ulti-
> mates are we entitled to embark on certain things. So that at
> least as a restraining force the point of view I brought in may
> be of some relevance.

To this, naturally, Arendt gives her assent.
   In the end, Arendt adopts a decidedly skeptical attitude toward the capabilities and limits of mental life. Thinking, we are
told, "does not create values; it will not find out, once and for all,
what 'the good' is; it does not confirm but, rather, dissolves ac-
cepted rules of conduct."[56] Thinking is Socratic, that is to say
negative; it destroys unexamined assumptions rather than dis-
covers truths. It is enough if we can succeed in reconciling ourselves to the way things are, for which purpose judging is indispensable, since it allows us to extract a modicum of pleasure
from the contingencies of life and the free deeds of men.

7. *The Unwritten Treatise*

> Life, said Pythagoras, is like a festival; just as some come to
> the festival to compete, some to ply their trade, but the best
> people come as spectators, so in life the slavish men go
> hunting for fame or gain, the philosophers for truth.
>
> Diogenes Laertius

AMONG THOSE who have closely and sympathetically followed
the progress of Hannah Arendt's thought, it is a commonly held
view that her theory of judging would have been the culmination
of her life's work and that this final chapter of her philosophy
would have provided an answer to many of the unresolved
problems of preceding chapters. J. Glenn Gray's observation,
quoted earlier, is a typical one:

> For those who knew her mind with some intimacy it was evident
> that she regarded judging to be her particular strength and in a
> real sense a hoped-for resolution of the impasse to which the
> reflections on willing seemed to lead her. As Kant's *Critique of
> Judgment* enabled him to break through some of the antin-
> omies of the earlier critiques, so she hoped to resolve the
> perplexities of thinking and willing by pondering the nature
> of our capacity for judging.[57]

But what is this "impasse" to which Gray refers, and how is
judging supposed to resolve the impasse?

To answer this question, we must turn back briefly to the point
at which Arendt's explorations had arrived by the end of the
Willing volume. The problem that was central to *Willing* concerned the nature of human freedom. The question Arendt asks
is: How can something as radically contingent and ephemeral as
the faculty of willing provide a sustainable basis for human freedom? In other words, how can men affirm their worldly condition if freedom has its source in something as private and indi-
vidualizing as the human will? Throughout her writings Arendt
had consistently characterized freedom as something essentially
worldly and public, related to the tangible world of political
action. But in her final work she traces freedom as action in a
public world to the spontaneity, contingency, and autonomy of
the will. This culminates in her invoking the Augustinian notion
of natality, "the fact that human beings, new men, again and
again appear in the world by virtue of birth." "That there be a

beginning, man was created, before whom nobody was."[58] The problem is that this prospect of absolute spontaneity, absolute beginning, is not exactly easy for men to face up to, nor is it something they can comfortably embrace. Thus we commonly find even the men of action drawing back from their own revolutionary initiatives, seeking out precedents or historical sanction to mitigate the unconditional novelty of their deeds. Thus willing, even as depicted in the most favorable light— in Augustine's image of the miraculousness of natality—still carries an implication of compulsion rather than positive attraction. After all, we do not choose to be born; it is something that befalls us, whether we like it or not. The problem remains: How to affirm freedom? The will, with its radical contingency, offers no compelling answer. Arendt describes this as an "impasse," and she turns to the faculty of judging as the only way out of this impasse. The notion that we are *born* to freedom suggests somehow that we are merely fated or, worse, "doomed" to be free. Judging, by contrast, allows us to experience a sense of positive pleasure in the contingency of the particular. Arendt's thought here is that human beings have commonly felt the "awesome responsibility" of freedom to be an insupportable weight, which they have sought to evade by various doctrines, such as fatalism or the idea of historical process, and that the only way in which human freedom can actually be affirmed is by eliciting pleasure from the free acts of men by reflecting upon and judging them; ·and this, for Arendt, comes to pass quintessentially in the telling of stories and the writing of human history. Politics, in her view, is ultimately justified by the stories that are told afterwards. Human action is redeemed by retrospective judgment.

To place Arendt's problem in its proper context, it may help to recall very briefly the problem of freedom as it is posed in Kant's three *Critiques*. From the perspective of the first *Critique*, the phenomenal world presents nothing but causal necessities for theoretical contemplation. Therefore, to keep freedom from being completely submerged by the faculty of theoretical reason, Kant houses freedom in the noumenal will of the practical subject. The problem here, however, is that freedom seems to bear no relation to goings-on in the phenomenal world, and it is preserved only on condition that it disappear from the sensible and visible world in which we dwell. Reflective judgment, as interpreted by Arendt, offers a form of contemplation that is not restricted to the beholding of necessities and, at the same time, is not divorced from the worldly phenomena of human action. Reflective judgment thus provides some measure of respite from the antinomy of freedom and nature that characterizes the first two *Critiques*.

Arendt's reflections on judging took the form of a commentary on Kant, owing to "the curious scarcity of sources providing authoritative testimony. Not till Kant's *Critique of Judgment* did this faculty become a major topic of a major thinker."[59] To open our discussion of this material, we shall briefly survey the sources in Kant's work that Arendt appropriates for her theory of judgment, providing a kind of extended paraphrase of what she seeks to draw from Kant's work.

Kant defined judging as an activity of subsuming particulars under a universal. He calls judgment "the faculty of thinking the particular,"[60] and to think a particular means of course to bring it under a general concept. Furthermore, Kant distinguished between two types of judging, one in which the universal (the rule, principle, or law) is given for the subsumption, and one in which the universal is lacking and must somehow be produced from the particular; the former he labeled "determinant," the latter "reflective."[61] This activity of judging occurs when we are confronted with a particular. It is not a question of rendering a general commentary on a given *kind* of object; rather, *this* particular object calls for judgment. Judgment is reasoning about particulars as opposed to reasoning about universals. In the act of subsuming a particular rose under the universal category "beauty," I do not judge it to be such because I have available to me a rule of the type "All flowers of such-and-such a species are beautiful." Rather, the particular rose before me somehow "generates" the predicate beauty. I can understand and apply the universal only through experiencing the kinds of particulars to which we attach this predicate. Aesthetic judgment, therefore, is a matter of judging *this* rose, and only by extension do we broaden it into a judgment about all roses.

Kant also held that the activity of judging (as explicated in the "Critique of Aesthetic Judgment") is inherently social, because our aesthetic judgments make reference to a common or shared world, to what appears in public to all judging subjects, and thus not merely to the private whims or subjective preferences of individuals. In matters of "taste" I never judge only for myself, for the act of judging always implies a commitment to communicate my judgment; that is, judgment is rendered with a view to persuading others of its validity. This effort at persuasion is not external to the judgment; rather, it supplies the very *raison d'être* of judging. This is because there is no epistemically secure procedure for achieving correspondence to the object judged short of consensus arrived at in the actual course of truth-seeking communication. Judgment is the mental process by which one projects oneself into a counterfactual situation of disinterested reflection in order to satisfy oneself and an imagined community of potential collocutors that a particular has been adequately appraised.[62]

Yet the objection might be made that political judgments—as well as aesthetic judgments—are merely relative, dependent on "the eye of the beholder." After all, the concept of "taste," which is the crucial one for Kant, refers in its primary signification to the kinds of judgment involved in, say, "the preference for clam chowder over pea soup."[63] Why should a more exalted meaning than this be accorded to "matters of taste" in either the aesthetic or the political realm? Why should one person's taste be considered better or worse than another's? And, if they are equally good, are they not then mutually irrelevant? It was to provide a satisfactory answer to such questions that Kant devoted his "Critique of Aesthetic Judgment" to the argument that aesthetic judgments (and, by extension, other kinds of judgment relating to things we all hold in common) are *not* subjectively relative or egoistic, although neither do they refer to a concept of the object that simply determines the judgment cognitively. Rather, Kant's account of taste implies a concept of "intersubjectivity," where the judgment concerned is neither strictly objective nor strictly subjective. Needless to say, Kant did not use the term "intersubjectivity." He called it "pluralism," which he defined in his *Anthropology* as "the attitude of not being occupied with oneself as the whole world, but regarding and conducting oneself as a citizen of the world."[64] Intersubjective judgment arises from what is held in common among the subjects, from what is—literally—*between* them; namely, what Kant in the definition just cited calls "the world." The "in-between" of judging subjects is the realm of objects fit for judgment, and we display taste in rendering judgment upon them. This display of taste is a social relation, for we are always already committed to seeking acknowledgment from our fellows, to get them to acknowledge the reasonableness or rationality of our judgment and, thereby, to confirm our own "good taste." Although our present concern is with aesthetics, one can extend the argument to show that this process of claiming and winning acknowledgment for our judgments is actually a general feature of human rationality.[65] In short, as a response to those who allege the relativity of judgments, we may aver that, in the words of Burke, "if there were not some principles of judgment as well as of sentiment common to all mankind, no hold could possibly be taken either on their reason or their passions, sufficient to maintain the ordinary correspondence of life."[66]

Let us now introduce some of the fundamental concepts of the "Critique of Aesthetic Judgment." Aesthetic taste for Kant is disinterested; contemplative rather than practical, autonomous rather than heteronomous, it is, in a word, *free*. What endows it with these qualities of disinterestedness, autonomy, and freedom is the ability of the aesthetic judge, critic, or spectator to rise above everyday interests by claiming an experience of aesthetic form to which all men can (in principle) give their assent. All men share the faculties of understanding and imagination, the formal interaction of which results in the ascription of beauty to aesthetic objects. Thus, as Kant puts it, "we are suitors for agreement from everyone else, because we are fortified with a ground common to all."[67] Kant calls this ground of shared judgment "common sense," which he characterizes not as a private feeling but as "a public sense."[68] Kant describes this process of claiming universal assent as follows: "The assertion is not that everyone *will* fall in with our judgment, but rather that everyone *ought* to agree with it. Here I put forward my judgment of taste as an example of the judgment of common sense, and attribute to it on that account *exemplary* validity."[69] I posit common sense as an "ideal norm" that demands universal assent, "the consensus of different judging subjects." The task that Kant sets for himself is to inquire into the basis for this ideally posited "consensus."

In the present context, the most important section of Kant's work is § 40 of the *Critique of Judgment,* entitled "Taste as a kind of *sensus communis.*" Kant writes that

> by the name of *sensus communis* is to be understood the idea of a *public* sense, i.e., a critical faculty which in its reflective act takes account (*a priori*) of the mode of representation of everyone else, in order, *as it were,* to weigh its judgment with the collective reason of mankind. . . . This is accomplished by weighing the judgment, not so much with actual, as rather

with the merely possible, judgments of others, and by putting
ourselves in the position of everyone else, as the result of a
mere abstraction from the limitations which contingently affect our own estimate.

Kant specifies three "maxims of common human understanding," which are: (1) Think for oneself; (2) Think from the
standpoint of everyone else; and (3) Always think consistently. It
is the second of these, which Kant refers to as the maxim of
enlarged thought, that concerns us here, for it is the one that,
according to Kant, belongs to judgment (the first and third apply
to understanding and reason, respectively). Kant observes that
we designate someone as a "man of *enlarged mind* . . . if he de-
taches himself from the subjective personal conditions of his
judgment, which cramp the minds of so many others, and reflects upon his own judgment from a *universal standpoint* (which
he can only determine by shifting his ground to the standpoint
of others)." Kant concludes that we can rightfully refer to
aesthetic judgment and taste as a *sensus communis,* or "public
sense." This particular discussion issues in the definition of taste
as "the faculty of estimating what makes our feeling in a given
representation *universally communicable* without the mediation of
a concept."
    To these concepts of common sense, consensus, and enlarged
mentality, let us add another, from Kant's short essay "What is
Enlightenment?"—namely, the concept of "public use of one's
reason." In the context of Kant's argument, the public use of
one's reason pertains particularly to the problem of freedom of
the press in the Age of Enlightenment. Kant's own problems
with the Prussian censor are well known. But what renders this
concept of considerably wider application is the idea that thinking *in public* can be constitutive of thinking *as such.* This insight
runs counter to widespread assumptions about the nature of
thinking, according to which thought can operate privately no
less well than publicly. Kant denies such assumptions, arguing
that public presentation of ideas, for public consideration and
debate—in his case, the right of the scholar to put his thought in
writing for the judgment of a reading public—is absolutely indispensable for the progress of enlightenment (not merely in the
sense that thoughts once arrived at should then be disseminated
as widely as possible, but in the deeper sense that exchange of
views on a universal basis *itself* contributes to the development of

those thoughts). Kant regards restriction of the *private* use of reason, as exercised in a particular civil post or office or before a private congregation, as a much less serious infringement of liberty than limitations on the scholar who addresses writings to an enlightened public. This precedence accorded to public over private prerogatives may appear as something of an inversion of traditional liberal priorities on the part of one of the leading fountainheads of liberal thought. But on this point Kant is unequivocal: the use of reason in addressing a domestic or private gathering is dispensable to freedom, whereas the right to publicity, the right freely to submit one's judgments for public testing before "a society of world citizens," is not dispensable but is utterly necessary for freedom, progress, and enlightenment. The public airing of judgments thus takes precedence over the private exchange of opinions. The predominant concern here is with a world, or a community of world citizens, to whom we appeal even more urgently than we do to those immediately around us. Judgment must be universal, and it must be public—must address itself to all men and be concerned with those public things that appear before and are visible to all men.

This draws us toward the next leading concept of Kant's theory of judgment, that of "the spectator." We have already mentioned that the paramount qualities of aesthetic judgment, as described in Kant's work, include its being disinterested, contemplative, and free from all practical interest. Accordingly, in Kant's aesthetic and political writings, the full prerogative of judgment is granted to the spectator who stands back from the work of art, or stands back from political action, and reflects disinterestedly. In Kant's "pragmatic anthropology" his position is more ambiguous, since it would seem evident that the man of practice too, in making moral and prudential choices, exercises reflective judgment and taste. However, the guiding model or paradigm in Kant's work is that the genius first produces the work of art, and only then is it submitted to the taste of the critic. Judgment is retrospective and is pronounced by the bystander or onlooker, not by the artist himself. Correspondingly, only the political spectator, removed from the action, can render disinterested judgment on the human significance of events unfolding in the political world. The major political event that unfolded in Kant's own time, was, of course, the French Revolution, and he did not fail to apply his theory of judgment to this particular experience.

In his fascinating commentary on the French Revolution in
Part II of *The Contest of the Faculties* ("An Old Question Raised
Again: Is the Human Race Constantly Progressing?"), Kant
specifically emphasizes that his concern is not with the actual
deeds of the political agents but only with

> the mode of thinking of the spectators which reveals itself
> publicly in this game of great revolutions, and manifests such
> a universal yet disinterested sympathy for the players on one
> side against those on the other, even at the risk that this par-
> tiality could become very disadvantageous for them if dis-
> covered. Owing to its universality, this mode of thinking
> demonstrates a character of the human race at large and all at
> once; owing to its disinterestedness, a moral character of hu-
> manity, at least in its predisposition.[70]

Kant then declares that in spite of all the atrocities that render
the French Revolution morally and *practically* objectionable, "this
revolution nonetheless finds in the hearts of all spectators (who
are not engaged in this game themselves) a wishful participation
that borders closely on enthusiasm, the very expression of which
is fraught with danger." Kant explains that it is enthusiasm for
the pure concept of right that accounts for the exaltation with
which "the uninvolved public looking on sympathized without
the least intention of assisting."[71] It is worth noting that the two
qualities by which Kant here distinguishes political judgment—
namely, universality and disinterestedness—are the very same
two outstanding marks of judgment ascribed by Kant to aesthetic
taste. This famous passage shows unmistakably that political
judgment, like aesthetic judgment, is reserved to the spectator.[72]

Other passages in the works of Kant confirm this conception
of political judgment. For instance, in an early work, *Observations
on the Beautiful and Sublime,* Kant remarks that ambition, as an
attendant impulse, is most admirable (as long as it does not subordinate the other inclinations). "For since each one pursues
actions on the great stage according to his dominating inclinations, he is moved at the same time by a secret impulse to
take a standpoint outside himself in thought, in order to judge
the outward propriety of his behaviour as it seems in the eyes of
the onlooker."[73]

Arendt affirms this concept of judgment. For her, judging—
like thinking—entails a withdrawal from the "doings" of men in
order to reflect on the meaning of what they do. Arendt argues
in support of Kant that the actors in a political drama have only a

partial view (by definition, since they can enact only their own "parts") and that therefore the "meaning of the whole" is available only to the spectator.[74] Furthermore, as she elaborates in the Kant Lectures, there would be no point to the spectacle if the spectator were not accorded the primary role. She writes:

> We . . . are inclined to think that in order to judge a spectacle you must first have the spectacle—that the spectator is secondary to the actor; we tend to forget that no one in his right mind would ever put on a spectacle without being sure of having spectators to watch it. Kant is convinced that the world without man would be a desert, and a world without man means for him: without spectators.[75]

Kant in one place observes that in the drama of human history the spectator must discern a meaning, for otherwise he will tire of the never-ending farce. But only the *spectator* of history will tire of it, not the historical actors, "for the actors are fools" (since, as Arendt explains, they see only a part of the action, whereas the spectator views the whole).[76] "It may perhaps be moving and instructive to watch such a drama for a while; but the curtain must eventually descend." The spectator tires of it, "for any single act will be enough for him if he can reasonably conclude from it that the never-ending play will be of eternal sameness."[77] This is not the only instance in which Kant portrays judgment as a wearisome and melancholy business. In the *Anthropology* he specifically contrasts judgment with wit, on the grounds that judgment "limits our concepts and contributes more to correcting than to enlarging them. It is serious and rigorous, and limits our freedom in thinking. So, while we pay it all honour and commend it, it is unpopular." Wit is like play: "Judgment's activity is more like business.—Wit is more the bloom of youth: judgment, the ripe fruit of age." "Wit is interested in the sauce: judgment, in the solid food."[78] This passage echoes Burke, who likewise concludes that, compared to wit, the task of judgment is "more severe and irksome."[79] And in Kant's portraits of the various human temperaments in his *Observations,* it is the melancholy man who is distinguished chiefly by his uncompromising judgment: "He is a strict judge of himself and others, and not seldom is weary of himself as of the world. . . . He is in danger of becoming a visionary or a crank."[80] (To which Arendt adds: "[This] is certainly a self-portrait.")[81]

Arendt contends that Kant's desperate search for a way to escape the melancholy induced by the activity of judging gave rise to a grave tension within his theory of political judgment. One means of escape is through the idea of human progress, or the notion that history has a meaning. According to Arendt, however, this postulate contradicts the absolute supremacy accorded to the disinterested spectator, who is autonomous and therefore stands wholly independent of the actual course of history. This view becomes especially clear when we arrive at the closing paragraph of the Kant Lectures:

> We were talking about the partiality of the actor, who, because he is involved, never sees the meaning of the whole. This is true for all stories; Hegel is entirely right that philosophy, like the owl of Minerva, spreads its wings only when the day is over, at dusk. The same is not true for the beautiful or for any deed in itself. The beautiful is, in Kantian terms, an end in itself because all its possible meaning is contained within itself, without reference to others—without linkage, as it were, to other beautiful things. In Kant himself there is this contradiction: Infinite Progress is the law of the human species; at the same time, man's dignity demands that he be seen (every single one of us) in his particularity and, as such, be seen—but without any comparison and independent of time—as reflecting mankind in general. In other words, the very idea of progress—if it is more than a change in circumstances and an improvement of the world—contradicts Kant's notion of man's dignity. It is against human dignity to believe in progress. Progress, moreover, means that the story never has an end. The end of the story itself is in infinity. There is no point at which we might stand still and look back with the backward glance of the historian.[82]

In the light of these concluding sentences, we can begin to make sense of Arendt's two epigraphs, the first of which (also quoted at the very end of the *"Postscriptum"* to *Thinking*) translates: "The victorious cause pleased the gods, but the defeated one pleases Cato." The second, taken from Goethe's *Faust,* Part II, Act V, lines 11404–7, may be rendered thus: "If I could remove the magic from my path, / And utterly forget all enchanted spells, / Nature, I would stand before you as but a man, / Then it would be worth the effort of being a man." (The line preceding these reads as follows: "Noch hab' ich mich ins Freie nicht gekämpft"—"I have not won my way to freedom yet." The verse must, then, be read in accordance with the general intention already characterized at the beginning of this section.) The import of Arendt's first epigraph, at least, should be visible: The "miracles" of history give disinterested "pleasure" to the historical spectator. One may think of those episodes of political history, all of them ill-fated, where hope flickered briefly: the revolutionary councils of the Paris Commune of 1871, the Russian *soviets* of 1905 and 1917, the German and Bavarian *Räte* of 1918–19, the Hungarian uprising of 1956, each of which Arendt is so fond of citing.[83] Among these "miraculous" moments, entirely unpredictable and free, even if doomed to failure, we may include the Warsaw Ghetto resistance: "Not one of us will leave here alive. We are fighting not to save our lives but for human dignity."[84] For Arendt, the judging spectator—the historian, the poet, the storyteller—rescues these unique episodes from the oblivion of history, thereby salvaging a portion of human dignity, which would otherwise be denied to the participants in these doomed causes.

Events of this kind possess what Arendt, following Kant, calls "exemplary validity." By attending to the particular *qua* particular, in the form of an "example," the judging spectator is able to illuminate the universal without thereby reducing the particular to universals. The example is able to take on universal meaning while *retaining* its particularity, which is not the case when the particular serves merely to indicate a historical "trend." Only in this way can human dignity be upheld.

In the same light, I offer an exegesis of the second, more elusive, epigraph. What the two have in common is their concern for human worth or dignity. It is impossible to interpret the German verse with complete confidence, but I can perhaps render the meaning it had for Arendt as follows: The worth or dignity of man demands the removal of what, in *The Life of the Mind*, are called "the metaphysical fallacies," the most pernicious of which is the metaphysical idea of History. Judgment is rendered not by the collective destiny of mankind but by the "man alone," the judging spectator who stands before nature unencumbered by metaphysical dreams and illusions. His judgment is more decisive for the securing of human dignity than even the absolute fulfillment of history, as envisioned by Hegel or Marx, would be. Not History, but the historian, is the ultimate judge.

Let us now see whether we can begin to fit "Judging" within the context of the life of the mind as a whole, to give us some indication of its significance within the overall structure of Arendt's philosophy. Arendt's work *The Human Condition* is misleadingly named, since it actually deals with only half of the human condition, the *vita activa*. Indeed, Arendt herself titled this work *Vita Activa*, reserving the other half of the human condition, the *vita contemplativa*, for later treatment.[85] When Arendt finally returns to the half-completed project in her last work, she substitutes for the *vita contemplativa* the more general term "life of the mind." There is little of the contemplative in willing, and even thinking and judging, since they are said to be mental activities proper to every man, are denied the exclusive prerogative previously enjoyed by the contemplative men of philosophy and metaphysics. *The Life of the Mind* is modeled on the three critiques of Kant, for whom contemplation had ceased to be the ultimate standard of human existence. Thoughtful reflection, speculation, the raising of unanswerable questions, and the search for meaning are not the monopoly of the contemplative man, as traditionally conceived, but extend to the common reach of mankind, to the extent that men exercise their properly human faculties. Thus the question that Arendt addresses in *The Life of the Mind* is this: What are these characteristically human activities or faculties of the mind? What are the natural abilities, capacities, and potentialities of the thinking, willing, and judging ego, as disclosed by the phenomenology of mental life?

Like *The Human Condition*, *The Life of the Mind* was conceived as a trilogy, "Judging" constituting the third part, after *Thinking* and *Willing*. It is therefore important to understand and appreciate the relationship among the three parts of *The Life of the Mind*. According to Arendt, the three mental activities are autonomous, not only with respect to each other but with respect to other faculties of the mind as well.[86]

> Thinking, willing, and judging are the three basic mental activities; they cannot be derived from each other and though they have certain common characteristics they cannot be reduced to a common denominator.

> I called these mental activities basic because they are autonomous; each of them obeys the laws inherent in the activity itself.

> In Kant, it is reason with its "regulative ideas" that comes to the help of judgment; but if the faculty is separate from other faculties of the mind, then we shall have to ascribe to it its own *modus operandi*, its own way of proceeding.[87]

Arendt is especially concerned to establish the autonomy of these activities vis-à-vis intellect, for subordination of thinking, willing, and judgment to intellectual cognition would be to forfeit the freedom of the thinking, willing, and judging ego. In the *Thinking* volume, this autonomy is asserted by means of the distinction between truth and meaning. In the *Willing* volume, it is achieved by counterposing Duns Scotus to Aquinas and by suggesting that the former had a deeper insight into the phenomenology of the will than the latter. In what I surmise would have been the account of "Judging," the same objective would have been accomplished by affirming Kant's dichotomy between the noncognitive operation of reflective judgment and the cognitive operation of intellect. This would explain why Arendt ends the section on *Willing* by stating that an analysis of the faculty of Judgment "at least may tell us what is involved in our pleasures and displeasures."[88] She also points out that in neither of the two parts of the *Critique of Judgment* does Kant speak of man as a cognitive being: "The word truth does not occur."[89] In the same vein, she writes that cognitive propositions "are not judgments, properly speaking."[90] Judgment arises from the representation, not of what we know, but of what we feel.

This account clearly conflicts with some of her earlier formulations. In particular, there is a curious passage in "What is Freedom?" where action is said to stand in the following relation to will, judgment, and intellect:

> The aim of action varies and depends upon the changing circumstances of the world; to recognize the aim is not a matter of freedom, but of right or wrong judgment. Will, seen as a distinct and separate human faculty, follows judgment, i.e., cognition of the right aim, and then commands its execution. The power to command, to dictate action, is not a matter of freedom but a question of strength or weakness.
>
> Action insofar as it is free is neither under the guidance of the intellect nor under the dictate of the will—although it needs both for the execution of any particular goal.[91]

In this account, action, but not will, is said to be free, and judgment is associated with the intellect (as it was for Aquinas). In her later formulation, by contrast, will and judgment are both seen to be free—which, for Arendt, means not subordinate to intellect.[92]

"Judging" (or what we are able to reconstruct of it) is inte-

grally bound up with *Thinking* and *Willing*. All three are in-
tensely concerned with concepts of time and history. The time-
concept of *Thinking* is an "enduring present"; that of *Willing* is
future-oriented.[93] The growing ascendancy of the faculty of the
will (as documented by Heidegger) occasions the modern concept of historical progress, which in turn poses a threat to the
faculty of judging, for judging depends on a genuine relation to
the *past*. To the extent that we embrace a notion of mankind's
progress and thereby subordinate the particular (event) to the
universal (course of history), to that extent we relinquish the
dignity that comes from judging the particular in itself, apart
from its relation to the universal history of mankind. (It is in this
context that Arendt invokes Kant's idea of exemplary validity,
where the example discloses generality without surrendering
particularity.)

On a first reading, it is not easy to discern how the various
themes of the Kant Lectures hang together. Consider, once
again, the closing words of the manuscript: To believe in progress means that "there is no point at which we might stand still
and look back with the backward glance of the historian." Why
do the lectures break off precisely here? Were Arendt's reflections merely *interrupted* at this point, and would they have
been continued beyond this point when she resumed work on
"Judging"? Or can an underlying coherence be established, one
that allows us to see this as a natural endpoint and to surmise
that the finished version would have struck a similar note at its
close? I would maintain that, if we read the last lines of *Thinking*
with care, the internal structure of "Judging" will become clear
to us and will make perfect sense of the closing lines of the version
available to us.

In the *Postscriptum* to *Thinking,* Arendt writes:

> Finally we shall be left with the only alternative there is in
> these matters. Either we can say with Hegel: *Die Weltgeschichte
> ist das Weltgericht,* leaving the ultimate judgment to Success, or
> we can maintain with Kant the autonomy of the minds of men
> and their possible independence of things as they are or as
> they have come into being.
> Here we shall have to concern ourselves, not for the first
> time, with the concept of history. . . . [The] Homeric historian
> is the *judge.* If judgment is our faculty for dealing with the
> past, the historian is the inquiring man who by relating it sits
> in judgment over it. If that is so, we may reclaim our human

dignity, win it back, as it were, from the pseudo-divinity
named History of the modern age, without denying history's
importance but denying its right to be the ultimate judge. Old
Cato . . . has left us a curious phrase, which aptly sums up the
political principle implied in the enterprise of reclamation.
He said: "*Victrix causa deis placuit, sed victa Catoni*" ("The victorious cause pleased the gods, but the defeated one pleases
Cato").[94]

For Arendt, the ultimate alternative in deciding on a theory of
judgment is between Kant and Hegel—between autonomy and
history (with the proviso that Kant himself actually faltered between these alternatives).[95] A concept of judgment is ultimately
bound up with a concept of history. If history is progressive,
judgment is infinitely postponed. If there is an end to history,
the activity of judging is precluded. If history is neither progressive nor has an end, judgment redounds to the individual historian, who bestows meaning on the particular events or "stories"
of the past.

The *Postscriptum* indicates that the Kant Lectures reflect the
full intended structure of "Judging," since it makes clear that the
ultimate destination of "Judging" would be a return to the concept of history—and that, in fact, is where the Kant Lectures
terminate.

8. *Critical Questions*

THUS FAR I HAVE ATTEMPTED to make sense of the internal
structure of Arendt's thoughts on "judging." I now wish to confront certain problems in order to clear the way for a critical
assessment. First of all, let me summarize the essential elements
of a Kantian contribution to a theory of political judgment.
There is, to begin with, the distinction between reflective and
determinant judgment, as formulated in the Introduction to the
Critique of Judgment and defined also in Kant's *Logic*. Second,
there are the concepts of enlarged mentality, disinterestedness,
sensus communis, etc., as developed in the "Critique of Aesthetic
Judgment," especially §§ 39 and 40. Third, there is the notion of
the spectator, as it emerges in the discussion of the French Revolution in *Contest of the Faculties* (Part II: "An Old Question
Raised Again"); this concept of the spectator also appears in
Kant's *Observations on the Beautiful and Sublime* and elsewhere.

Fourth, there is the rather lengthy treatment of social taste in Kant's *Anthropology from a Pragmatic Point of View,* a work that also contains a detailed analysis of the cognitive faculties of reason, understanding, and judgment and a commentary on the distinction between wit and judgment, borrowed from some of the English empiricists. Fifth, there is the idea of the "public use of reason," the clearest expression of which is to be found in the short essay "What is Enlightenment?" Finally, there are scattered remarks about judgment in Kant's other works, such as his essay on "Theory and Practice" and his treatise *Education.* These, then, are the sources for formulating a Kantian approach to political judgment. But the question arises: Is Kant the only, or even the best, source for a theory of judgment? And is judgment the single irreducible or "autonomous" faculty that Arendt believes it to be and for an account of which she appeals exclusively to Kant? Or does this term take in a wide range of different capacities, exercised in a multiplicity of ways?

Before pursuing these questions, it might help to recapitulate the theory of judgment offered in the *Critique of Judgment.* Kant's theory is difficult and at times perplexing, but his account of aesthetic judgment is, in very rough outline, as follows: All human beings possess two faculties, the faculty of imagination and the faculty of understanding. The faculty of imagination corresponds to the sense of freedom; the faculty of understanding corresponds to the sense of conformity-to-rule. When we represent to ourselves the form of an aesthetic object in what Kant calls an act of "reflection" (as opposed to immediate apprehension of the object), certain formal features of the representation cause these two faculties to fall into harmony with each other, and this in turn generates a sense of pleasure in the subject. Thus the judgment of taste, as opposed to the judgment of sense, is "reflective," because, while it refers to the feeling of pleasure and displeasure evoked in the subject, this pleasure arises from a second-order representation that is not limited to experience of the object as immediately pleasing but, rather, "re-flects," or turns back upon, the object of our experience. The pleasure on which aesthetic judgment is based is a mediated or second-order pleasure, arising out of reflection; it is not immediate gratification. Since all human subjects possess the two faculties whose relation of harmony gives rise to this pleasure, we can rightly expect others to be capable of our experience of a given aesthetic form, just as we can try to project ourselves into their experience of it. This of course does not mean that we should expect that they *will* actually assent to our judgment; it means only that they *ought* to, if they purged themselves of extraneous influences and made the requisite effort to see the object from other points of view. According to Kant, there is no need to find actual alternative judgments, for we can reflect on the potential alternative standpoints by exercising *imagination*. We imagine how things *would* look from other perspectives without actually being presented with them in fact. This appeal to "enlarged mentality" fails when we are unable to free ourselves from "the limitations which contingently affect our own estimate."[96] In other words, a failure of aesthetic imagination is ascribed to an immersion in "empirical interests," in which the judgment of taste is overwhelmed by the judgment of sense, or mere gratification.

It may be objected that this account seems excessively formal and appears to address only a very narrow range of aesthetic experience (being more appropriate, for instance, to sculpture and painting than to drama; to poetry than to other forms of literature, such as the novel; to photography than to the cinema), but this objection is diminished when the account is considered in the light of the *purposes* a Kantian "critique" of judgment is intended to serve. Kant is concerned with an inquiry into the conditions of the *possible validity* of aesthetic judgments. He sets up the question by asking, Given that we sometimes make valid aesthetic judgments, *how is this possible?* He answers: "We are suitors for agreement from everyone else because we are fortified with a ground common to all."[97] The specification of this common ground requires a highly formal inquiry into human cognitive faculties (although taste is not regarded by Kant as itself a cognitive faculty, since it refers not to what we know but to what we feel). Provided that he can show *some* basis for shared judgment (however formal), he will have succeeded in securing a transcendental foundation for the possible validity of judgments of taste. The fact that *some* of our judgments operate in a quite different fashion in no way contradicts or is incompatible with Kant's project of justifying or legitimating the claims of taste.

In short, Kant offers a highly formalized account of what it is to judge because he is concerned not with substantive features of this or that judgment but, rather, with universal conditions of the possible validity of our judgments. The idea of applying such an account to politics is somewhat curious yet not altogether unintelligible. Political events are public, disclose themselves to the gaze of the apprehending spectator, and constitute a realm of appearances suitable for reflection. Politics, construed phenomenologically, evokes both imagination's freedom and the understanding's conformity-to-rule. A theory as formal as this may not prove sufficient for conceptualizing political judgment, but it does certainly provide a very interesting stimulus to further thought.

Now to consider some of the difficulties. First of all, we may note the conspicuous absence from Kant's account of, on the one hand, any attention to the kinds of knowledge involved in judgment and, on the other hand, any specification of epistemic capacities that render men qualified, in a greater or lesser degree, to judge—for instance, the whole dimension of judgment that we associate with the notion of prudence. Nowhere in Kant's discussion of judgment do we find a concern with the qualities of experience, maturity, and sound habituation that have traditionally been observed as the mark of practical wisdom in a man of action. Prudence was explicitly excluded by Kant from practical reason, for reasons deeply bound up with his moral philosophy. Although his moral philosophy and political philosophy are in many respects in mutual tension, Kant's rejection of prudence is carried over into his political thought, with the consequence that he deems experience to be quite irrelevant to political judgment on the grounds that politics is not about empirical happiness but about self-evident and indisputable rights.[98] He conceived of prudence as a species of technical-practical rules of art and skill—in particular, rules governing the skill involved in exercising an influence over men and subordinating their will to one's own.[99] Thus he classified it among what he termed "hypothetical imperatives"; for example, if it is given that I want a certain end, prudence determines the instrumental means by which I can achieve that end. In Kant's terms, this is a quasi-theoretical, not a genuinely practical, capacity, and it serves to reduce prudence to a *technē*, in Aristotle's sense. *Prudentia,* we may recall, was the Latin term used by Aquinas for Aristotle's *phronēsis* (which, unlike mere *technē*, comprehends the full dimensions of ethical deliberation and the determination of proper human ends). Therefore, if we wished to test the sufficiency of a Kantian theory of judgment, we would have to go back to Book VI of Aristotle's *Nicomachean Ethics,* for it is from there that we must trace the source of the term prudence, or *phronēsis.* Customarily translated as "practical wisdom," *phronēsis* is the centerpiece of Book VI, around which all the other concepts discussed—*epistēmē, technē, nous, sophia,* political *epistēmē,* deliberation, understanding, judgment, *aretē*—gravitate and to which they are all related, by way of both comparison and contrast. The confrontation of Aristotle with Kant raises the following very serious questions. First, does the spectator possess a monopoly of judgment, or does the political agent, too, exercise a faculty of judging? And, if the latter, how is the burden of judgment distributed between actor and spectator? Second, is disinterestedness the decisive criterion of judgment, or are other criteria, such as prudence, equally requisite? This links up with the question of teleology (in the Aristotelian, not Kantian, sense) and the relationship between aesthetic judgment and purposive judgment. Kant, as we have seen, regards aesthetic judgment as purely contemplative, divorced from any practical interest. Accordingly, a judgment of taste must abstract from any consideration of *ends;* aesthetic judgment must make no reference to teleology. But can *political* judgments abstract from practical ends, and is a strictly nonteleological conception of political judgment coherent? This, in turn, gives rise to further questions. For instance, what is the status of rhetoric within political judgment, and are the two necessarily related? Because Kant expels teleology from judgments of taste, he condemns rhetoric, since it corrupts aesthetics with the pursuit of ends.[100] But if the pursuit of ends is inseparable from, and indeed constitutive of, political as opposed to aesthetic judgment, is not rhetoric, too, in a constitutive relation to political judgment? Some of Aristotle's most important reflections on political judgment are contained in his treatise on *Rhetoric;* again one is confronted with questions about the sufficiency of the Kantian theory.

Kant also excludes from taste what he calls "empirical interests," such as social inclinations and passions. He offers the example of "charms," which are valued for their social attraction.[101] Charms, for Kant, are not subject to aesthetic judgment, which must be *a priori* and purely formal, not a product of mere sensation. Thus the aesthetic object must be appraised as to its form, apart from any sentiments of love or sympathy that it may evoke. Similarly, appealing to the judgment of one's fellows is, in the account Kant gives of it, a purely formal appeal, having nothing at all to do with any substantive relations of community (hence he speaks repeatedly of judgment being exercised *a priori*).[102] In judging the configuration of forms offered to mental reflection by an aesthetic object, I claim the assent of humanity as such (regarded as a formal judging community),[103] not that of any particular society. The substantive needs, purposes, and particular ends of my own community are as strictly irrelevant to the judgment as those of any other. This set of issues is posed most sharply in Hans-Georg Gadamer's critique of Kantian aesthetics. In Part I of *Truth and Method,* Gadamer claims that Kant "depoliticizes" the idea of *sensus communis,* which formerly had important political and moral connotations. According to Gadamer, Kant's formal and narrowed concept of judgment empties the older, Roman-rooted, conception of the very full moral-political content it once had. Kant, as it were, strips "common sense" of the richness of its *Roman* meaning. As countermodels to Kant, Gadamer cites Vico, Shaftesbury, and, above all, Aristotle. From Gadamer's Aristotelian standpoint, Kant "intellectualizes" the *sensus communis;* "aestheticizes" the faculty of taste, which had previously been understood as a social-moral faculty; very narrowly circumscribes and delimits the range of these concepts, including the concept of judgment; and generally abstracts these concepts from all relationships of community. Thus, if we wish to explore other possible sources of a theory of political judgment, one very promising avenue of inquiry is offered by Gadamer's philosophical hermeneutics, which presents a theory of hermeneutical judgment that eschews Kant and appeals to Aristotle's ethics.

As we have seen, Arendt states quite categorically that judging is not a cognitive faculty.[104] This prompts us to investigate the question whether reflective judgment is strictly noncognitive, or whether it unavoidably involves claims to truth. In contrast to a theory of judgment derivable from Aristotle, a Kantian theory of political judgment would not allow one to speak of political knowledge or political wisdom. The problem with this exclusion of knowledge from political judgment is that it renders one incapable of speaking of "uninformed" judgment and of distinguishing differential capacities for knowledge so that some persons may be recognized as more qualified, and some as less qualified, to judge. This point can be elaborated in connection with an objection that Jürgen Habermas leveled against Arendt in his well-argued critique in "Hannah Arendt's Communications Concept of Power":

Arendt sees a yawning abyss between knowledge and opinion that cannot be closed with arguments.

> She holds fast to the classical distinction between theory and practice; practice rests on opinions and convictions that cannot be true or false in the strict sense. . . . An antiquated concept of theoretical knowledge that is based on ultimate insights and certainties keeps Arendt from comprehending the process of reaching agreement about practical questions as rational discourse.[105]

Habermas argues that Arendt, by refusing to bring practical discourse within the ambit of rational discourse, denies it cognitive status and thereby severs knowledge from practical judgment. Arendt's claim is that to specify a cognitive foundation for political beliefs (which Habermas seeks to do) would compromise the integrity of opinion. However, it is not clear how we could make sense of opinions that did not involve *any* cognitive claims (and therefore, by implication, truth-claims that are potentially corrigible) or why we should be expected to take seriously opinions that assert no claims to truth (or do not at least claim *more* truth than is claimed by available alternative opinions). It would seem that *all* human judgments, including aesthetic (and certainly political) judgments, incorporate a necessary cognitive dimension. A rigid dichotomy between the cognitive and the noncognitive, excluding any cognitive dimension from aesthetic judgment, seems to neglect the "reflective" element that pertains even to cognitive judgments (the elements of discretion or "judgment" in a reflective sense required for problematical cognitive judgments); it also appears to neglect the extent to which even, say, aesthetic judgments depend on cognitive discriminations and cognitive insights (as, for instance, when our appreciation of a painting is enhanced by our *knowing* that it belongs to a certain period).

   Kant, as we have seen, offers a highly formal account of judging. This is acceptable insofar as what is sought is a transcendental deduction of the faculty of taste. But at some point one must ask: What is it in the *content* of the ends and purposes of political actors or historical agents that makes this set of political appearances, rather than that set, worth attending to? What is it in the content of a given judgment that renders it an informed judgment, a reliable judgment, a practiced judgment, as

opposed to judgments that lack these attributes?[106] What, sub-
stantively, characterizes someone as discriminating or knowl-
edgeable or responsible in his judgments—apart from the *formal*
conditions of disinterestedness and freedom from extraneous
influences or heteronomous constraints? What are the *substantive*
conditions that allow us to acknowledge wisdom and experience
in the judging subject and appropriateness and relevance in the
object of judgment? Without at some point introducing questions like these, the attempt to transpose a theory of judging as
formal as Kant's into a theory of political judgment runs the risk
of turning from a genuine appreciation of political appearances
qua appearances into an unwarranted aestheticization of politics.
It is at this juncture that Arendt would have done well to consult
Aristotle, for he situates judgment firmly within the context of
the substantive ends and purposes of political deliberation,
rhetoric, and community.

   There are, as we have seen, various problems involved in
using Kant as the source of a theory of political judgment. However, to judge by her later formulations, this is not really what
Arendt seeks from Kant. Her objective is no longer a theory of
political judgment, for, as she now conceives the matter, there is
only *one* faculty of judgment, unitary and indivisible, which is
present in various circumstances—in the verdict of an aesthetic
critic, the verdict of a historical observer, the tragic verdict of a
storyteller or poet—and the variety of circumstance does not
relevantly affect the character of the faculty thus instantiated.
Hence there can be no distinct faculty that we might identify,
characteristically, as *political* judgment; there is only the ordinary
capacity of judgment, now addressing itself to political events (or
as Arendt would say, political appearances). This discloses a
deep tension between Arendt's earlier reflections on judgment
(as found in "The Crisis in Culture," "Truth and Politics," and
elsewhere) and what seemed to be emerging as her definitive
formulation. In the earlier formulations we find discussions of
the relation of judgment to "representative thinking" and opinion, leading one to suppose that judgment is a faculty exercised
by actors in political deliberation and action. (This, it had appeared, was what originally led Arendt to call judgment "the
most political of man's mental abilities," "one of the fundamental
abilities of man as a political being," the political faculty par
excellence.) But this approach is implicitly denied in her later

account. We have already mentioned that in "What is Freedom?" Arendt aligns judgment with intellect or cognition, in stark contrast to her eventual denial that judgment is an intellectual faculty or is indeed cognitive at all. In unpublished lectures delivered in 1965 and 1966, Arendt went to the opposite extreme, defining judgment as a function of the will (identifying it with the *liberum arbitrium*, the "arbitrating function" of the will). And in one context she even went so far as to say that "whether this faculty of judgment, one of the most mysterious faculties of the human mind, should be said to be the will or reason, *or perhaps a third mental capacity*, is at least an open question."[107] So we see that it was only gradually that Arendt came to regard judging as a separate mental activity, distinct from both intellect and will; and, by the time she had settled this question in her own mind, she had come to reformulate the very relation between judgment and politics—between "the life of the mind" and "the world of appearances."

The question is whether (and to what extent) judgment participates in the *vita activa* or whether it is confined, as a mental activity, to the *vita contemplativa*—a sphere of human life that Arendt conceived to be, by definition, solitary, exercised in withdrawal from the world and from other men. This fundamental uncertainty as to where judgment fits within the overall perspective is finally resolved by Arendt only by negating some of her own broader insights into judgment. On the one hand, she is tempted to integrate judgment into the *vita activa*, seeing it as a function of the representative thinking and enlarged mentality of political actors, exchanging opinions in public while engaged in common deliberation. On the other hand, she wants to emphasize the contemplative and disinterested dimension of judgment, which operates retrospectively, like aesthetic judgment. Judgment in the latter sense is placed exclusively within the ambit of the life of the mind. Arendt acheives a final resolution by abolishing this tension, opting wholly for the latter conception of judgment. This resolution ultimately produces consistency, but it is a strained consistency, achieved at the price of excluding any reference to the *vita activa* within the revised concept of judgment. The only point at which the exercise of judgment becomes practically efficacious, or even practically relevant, is in times of crisis or emergency: judgment "may prevent catastrophes, at least for myself, in the rare moments when the chips are down." Aside from these "rare moments," judgment pertains only to the life of the mind, the mind's communion with itself in solitary reflection.

Judgment is thus caught in the tension between the *vita activa* and the *vita contemplativa* (a dualism that pervades Arendt's entire work). Arendt tries to overcome this tension by placing judgment squarely within the life of the mind, yet it remains the mental faculty that verges most closely upon the worldly activities of man and (of the three powers of the mind) maintains the closest ties to those activities. By adhering to a firm disjunction between mental and worldly activities, Arendt was forced to expel judging from the world of the *vita activa,* to which it maintains a natural affinity. The upshot is that her more systematic reflection on the nature of judging resulted in a much narrower (and perhaps less rich) concept of judgment.[108]

At this point we return to our initial question and ask again: Is Kant our only source in these matters? Did Kant discover "an entirely new human faculty,"[109] previously unknown? No, unless one construes the faculty of judgment so narrowly that only someone with a theory of judgment identical to his would count as having been aware of it. At times, however, Arendt herself is willing to acknowledge that Kant did not hold an exclusive monopoly in this field. In particular, she notes in "The Crisis in Culture" that the recognition of judgment as a fundamental political ability of man rests on "insights that are virtually as old as articulated political experience. The Greeks called this ability *phronēsis,* or insight, and they considered it the principle virtue or excellence of the statesman in distinction from the wisdom of the philosopher." In note 14, accompanying this text, she then remarks: "Aristotle, who (*Nicomachean Ethics,* Book VI) deliberately set the insight of the statesman against the wisdom of the philosopher, was probably following, as he did so often in his political writings, the public opinion of the Athenian polis."[110] But if Arendt herself is willing to admit that Aristotle offers an alternative approach to a theory of judging, our question becomes even more pressing. We must inquire why she turned exclusively to Kant for inspiration when she sought to explore the theme of judgment (assuming that the converse does not hold—namely, that it was her lasting fascination with Kant that initially led her into a concern with judgment—which is of course quite possible).

No one well acquainted with Arendt's work can fail to appreciate the profound hold that Kant had on her thought. Kant provided not merely the source from which to appropriate a theory of judgment; for Arendt, he embodied her entire conception of the public, and he is in that sense her only true precursor. To grasp how Arendt could see in Kant's writings on judgment an anticipation of her own conception of politics, we must remember that, for Arendt, politics is a matter of judging appearances, not purposes. It is for this reason that she can assimilate political judgment to aesthetic judgment. Thus it is hardly fortuitous that Arendt turns to aesthetics for a model of political judgment; she had already assumed an affinity between politics and aesthetics, for both concern the world of appearances. And, as she writes: "In the work of no other philosopher has the concept of appearance . . . played so decisive and central a role as in Kant."[111] From this it follows, for Arendt, that he also possessed a unique awareness of the essence of the political.

In an earlier version of the Kant Lectures (1964), Arendt admits that, because of the old prejudices according to which politics was about rule or dominion, about interest, instrumentality, and so on, even Kant himself did not realize that the *Critique of Judgment* belonged to political philosophy. But in concerning ourselves with judgment, she holds, we break free of the old prejudices about politics: "We deal with a form of being together [shared judgment, community of taste] where no one rules and no one obeys. Where people persuade each other." And she continues: "This is not to deny that interest and power and rule . . . are very important and even central political concepts. . . . The question is: Are they the fundamental concepts, or are they derived from the living-together that itself springs from a different source? (Company—Action)."[112]

Arendt's view is that we are more likely to get at this other source by turning to a work whose explicit theme is "appearances *qua* appearances" than by concentrating on the works that make up the established tradition of political philosophy:

> The *Critique of Judgment* is the only [one of Kant's] great writings where his point of departure is the World and the senses and capabilities which made men (in the plural) fit to be inhabitants of it. This is perhaps not yet political philosophy, but it certainly is its condition *sine qua non*. If it could be found that in the capacities and regulative traffic and intercourse

between men who are bound to each other by the common
possession of a world (the earth) there exists an *a priori* principle, then it would be proved that man is essentially a political
being.[113]

At this point we may pause to consider a question that offers
perhaps the most obvious objection to Arendt's enterprise,
though it need not cause excessive concern; this is the question
whether Arendt takes undue liberties with Kant's texts. It is
undeniable that she is very free in her handling of Kant's work,
making use of his writings in accordance with her own purposes.
There is, for example, scarcely any reference to the *Critique of
Practical Reason* in lectures purporting to explicate his political
philosophy.[114] In an early essay she goes so far as to say that it
can "be seen from all his political writings that for Kant himself
the theme of 'judgment' carried more weight than that of 'practical reason.'"[115] Kant's writings on history are treated with a
similar latitude, with Arendt implying that Kant was just playing
games in his philosophy of history.[116] Clearly, this liberty with
Kant's written work is to some extent deliberate, for the claim
that he did not have a viable political philosophy serves to justify
Arendt's reconstruction of his unwritten political philosophy.
She thinks that Kant failed to develop fully the potential for a
political philosophy that is latent in the insights of the *Critique of
Judgment,* and she accordingly pushes the doctrines of that work
in the direction that is likely to fulfill this potential. In
downgrading the importance of his *actual* political writings (in
favor of the political philosophy that he did not write), Arendt
may have underestimated the importance of the political philosophy that Kant *did* write. Indeed, the Kantian version of
liberalism enjoys a growing appeal among liberal political philosophers in the present day (John Rawls and Ronald Dworkin
being the notable examples). However, in weighing this objection we should bear in mind that Arendt herself, more concerned with philosophical appropriation than scholarly fidelity,
is not unaware of the fact that she is interpreting Kant very
liberally.[117] She is quite ready to admit that what concerns her is
not his *actual* political philosophy but the political philosophy he
could have written had *certain* of his ideas been developed sys-
tematically.[118] There is nothing intrinsically objectionable about
such a procedure so long as one is clear that the enterprise is not
purely exegetical. As Heidegger, in his own work on Kant, remarks: "In contrast to the methods of historical philology, which

has its own problems, a dialogue between thinkers is bound by other laws."[119]

From what I have said thus far, it should be somewhat clearer why Arendt would immediately and most naturally turn to Kant for counsel on the question of judgment. But another, perhaps more subtle, reason suggests why Kant so dominated Arendt's thinking about judgment. For this, the decisive clue is provided by the one and only passage in *The Human Condition* that refers to the faculty of judgment:

> Where human pride is still intact, it is tragedy rather than absurdity which is taken to be the hallmark of human existence. Its greatest representative is Kant, to whom the spontaneity of acting, and the concomitant faculties of practical reason, including force of judgment, remain the outstanding qualities of man, even though his action falls into the determinism of natural laws and his judgment cannot penetrate the secret of absolute reality.[120]

Human judgment tends to be tragic judgment. It continually confronts a reality it can never fully master but to which it must nonetheless reconcile itself. Arendt finds in Kant a unique expression of this tragic quality associated with judgment. This helps us also to see why the image of the spectator is so vital and why the burden of judgment is conferred wholly upon the judging spectator. In history, as in drama, only retrospective judgment can reconcile men to tragedy:

> We may see, with Aristotle, in the poet's political function the operation of a catharsis, a cleansing or purging of all emotions that could prevent men from acting. The political function of the storyteller—historian or novelist—is to teach acceptance of things as they are. Out of this acceptance, which can also be called truthfulness, arises the faculty of judgment.[121]

Political judgment provides men with a sense of hope by which to sustain them in action when confronted with tragic barriers. Only the spectator of history is in a position to proffer such hope.[122] (This is in fact the preponderant message of Kant's explicitly political writings.) And if a concern with judgment leads one into an awareness of tragic imperatives, perhaps only a thinker with a full appreciation of those tragic realities (which Kant did indeed possess) could penetrate to, and capture in theoretical terms, the essence of judgment.

For Arendt the act of judging represents the culmination of the tripartite activity of the mind because, on the one hand, it maintains the contact with "the world of appearances" that is characteristic of "willing," and, on the other hand, it fulfills the quest for meaning that animates "thinking." Hence Arendt agrees with Pythagoras that in the festival of life "the best people come as spectators."[123] She departs from Pythagoras, however, in her denial that it is the truth-seeking of the philosophers that corresponds to this spectatorship. In her account, the contemplative function of the judging spectator supplants the discredited contemplative function of the philosopher or metaphysician.[124] The life of the mind reaches its ultimate fulfillment not in the comprehensive vision of a metaphysics, as it did for the ancients, but in the disinterested pleasure of the judging historian, poet, or storyteller.

9. Further Thoughts: Arendt and Nietzsche on "this gateway, Moment"

Evening judgment.—He who reviews his day's and life's work when he is weary and worn out, generally arrives at a melancholy conclusion: this, however, is not the fault of day and life, but of weariness. In the midst of our work, and even our pleasures, we usually find no leisure to muse over life and existence: but should this for once actually happen, we should no longer concede the point to him who was waiting for the seventh day and for rest to find all things in existence very beautiful—he had missed the right moment.

Nietzsche, *The Dawn of Day,* no. 317
(trans. Johanna Volz)

THE SAME STRUCTURE of thinking animates both Arendt's concept of judgment and Nietzsche's thought of eternal return; one might say that both arise from something like the same thought-experiment. Imagine a moment completely isolated from all others, all its possible meaning "contained within itself, without reference to others, *without linkage, as it were,*"[125] a moment of the most intense existential import. How can *this* moment, by itself, sustain the meaning of an entire life-existence? For Nietzsche this ontological anchoring is achieved through an anticipation of its infinite recurrence. For Arendt it is achieved through the backward glance of historical judgment.

Both thoughts derive fundamentally from the insight that the problem of meaning is coterminous with the problem of time, that the securing of a genuine sense of meaning hinges on the possibility of somehow overcoming the tyranny of time. (This is why the problem of the time dimensions of the mental faculties looms so large in *The Life of the Mind.*) Meaning must transcend time; it must be sheltered against the ravages of temporal flux. Unless the past can be recaptured (in an act of judgment), or unless there is the promise of its eventual return, all human life is rendered utterly meaningless and without point. Without ontological support for the moment against the flux of time, human life is indeed "like a leaf in the wind, a plaything of nonsense."[126]

In his very first book, *The Birth of Tragedy*, Nietzsche stated a problem that was to preoccupy him throughout his philosophical life; his ultimate solution for it was to be the thought of the eternal return. Arendt, also, constantly grappled with this problem; it prompted the reflection on political action that constitutes her book *The Human Condition*, and its ultimate solution lay, for her, in the idea of judging. The problem is how to meet the challenge of Silenus, found in Sophocles' play *Oedipus at Colonus:* "Not to be born prevails over all meaning uttered in words; by far the second-best thing is for life, once it has appeared, to go back as quickly as possible whence it came"—a challenge restated at the very end of Arendt's book *On Revolution* (as well as in the Kant Lectures themselves).[127] Arendt's first solution to this problem was, as we said, based on the concept of political action. As she put it in the last sentence of *On Revolution:* "it was the polis, the space of men's free deeds and living words, which could endow life with splendor"; it was this "that enabled ordinary men, young and old, to bear life's burden."[128] In her later works, however, another, though related, solution emerges. The political actor on his own cannot secure meaning; the actor needs a spectator. Hence the necessity of judgment. It is not politics alone that supports the moment against transient time; it is rather the act of judging on the part of a detached spectator, who reflects back on what the actor has done, on the "great words and deeds" of the past. It is in this light that Arendt interprets Goethe: "Nature, I would stand before you as but a man, / Then it would be worth the effort of being a man."

The aphorism in which Nietzsche first introduces the thought of the eternal return is entitled "The greatest stress":

How, if some day or night a demon were to sneak after you
into your loneliest loneliness and say to you, "This life as you
now live it and have lived it, you will have to live once more
and innumerable times more; and there will be nothing new
in it, but every pain and every joy and every thought and sigh
and everything immeasurably small or great in your life must
return to you—all in the same succession and sequence—even
this spider and this moonlight between the trees, and even
this moment and I myself. The eternal hourglass of existence
is turned over and over, and you with it, a dust grain of dust."
Would you not throw yourself down and gnash your teeth
and curse the demon who spoke thus? Or did you once experience a tremendous moment when you would have answered him, "You are a god, and never have I heard anything
more godly." If this thought were to gain possession of you, it
would change you, as you are, or perhaps crush you. The
question in each and every thing, "Do you want this once
more and innumerable times more?" would weigh upon your
actions as the greatest stress. Or how well disposed would you
have to become to yourself and to life to *crave nothing more
fervently* than this ultimate eternal confirmation and seal?[129]

For Nietzsche the decisive question is whether we are prepared to relive our life exactly as we have lived it, and to relive it
innumerable times. (Kant actually poses the very same question;
measured in terms of happiness, the value of life for us "is less
than nothing. For who would enter life afresh under the same
conditions?"[130] Kant's answer was that consciousness of our own
dignity as bearers of the moral law redeems an otherwise in-
tolerable existence; needless to say, Nietzsche had a very different answer to the question.) The thought of eternal return poses
this question in its starkest form—dramatizes it, as it were. Obviously, the overall achievements of our life in no way redeem
existence from the point of view of this question; if each moment
is to be relived innumerable times, the only way to endure this is
to embrace the eternity of the moment itself. If the moment is
incapable of absolutely justifying itself, there is no possibility of
wishing to relive it eternally by reference to what will happen at
some *other* point in the course of life. End, goal, telos, cease to be
relevant in the evaluation of human existence; thus the eternal
return has the effect of forcing the moment to answer for itself.

It may seem that what is at stake in Nietzsche's thought of the
eternal return is not the moment but the whole of time, "all in
the same succession and sequence." But this would be a misun-

derstanding, for it is by affirming the *moment* that we affirm all time. What allows one to bear "the greatest stress" is the experience of "a tremendous moment." (This distinction corresponds to Arendt's contrast between Hegelian *Weltgeschichte* as *Weltgericht* and Kantian *autonomy* of human judgment.) This becomes even clearer in Nietzsche's account of the eternal return in *Thus Spoke Zarathustra:*

> Behold . . . this moment! From this gateway, Moment, a long, eternal lane leads *backward:* behind us lies an eternity. Must not whatever *can* walk have walked on this lane before? Must not whatever *can* happen have happened, have been done, have passed by before? And if everything has been there before—what do you think, dwarf, of this moment? Must not this gateway too have been there before? And are not all things knotted together so firmly that this moment draws after it *all* that is to come? Therefore—itself too? For whatever *can* walk—in this long lane out *there* too, it *must* walk once more.
>
> And this slow spider, which crawls in the moonlight, and this moonlight itself, and I and you in the gateway, whispering together, whispering of eternal things—must not all of us have been there before?And return and walk in that other lane, out there, before us, in this long dreadful lane—must we not eternally return?[131]

It is true enough that Nietzsche here sees "all things knotted together so firmly" that the moment is anything but "without linkage, as it were," to other moments. On the other hand, however, affirmation is possible only on the basis of the moment:

> Behold this gateway, dwarf! . . . It has two faces. Two paths meet here; no one has yet followed either to its end. This long lane stretches back for an eternity. And the long lane out there, that is another eternity. They contradict each other, these paths; they offend each other face to face; and it is here at this gateway that they come together. The name of the gateway is inscribed above: "Moment." But whoever would follow one of them, on and on, farther and farther—do you believe, dwarf, that these paths contradict each other eternally?[132]

This passage is highly reminiscent of Kafka's parable, from the collection of aphorisms entitled "He," upon which Arendt lays such emphasis in *Thinking*. (Arendt actually quotes Nietzsche's "The Vision and the Riddle" in the context of her exegesis of Kafka in chapter 20 of *Thinking*, where she also cites Heidegger's commentary on Nietzsche, according to which eternity *is* in the moment because the two eternities are brought into collision only by the man in the gateway, the one who *himself is* the moment.[133] It is not fortuitous that Arendt herself cites this passage from *Zarathustra* in the last chapter of *Thinking* because the problem she is struggling with in *The Life of the Mind* replicates the very problem that induces Nietzsche to formulate the thought of eternal return.) Like the contradiction between two eternities in Nietzsche's account, Kafka's "He" is caught in a struggle between the past and future. To arbitrate this conflict, "He" must leap beyond this struggle, "jumping out of the fighting line to be promoted to the position of umpire, the spectator and judge outside the game of life, to whom the meaning of this time span between birth and death can be referred because 'he' is not involved in it."[134] This is the position of Arendt's judging spectator, caught in "the gap between past and future," as she puts it.

> In this gap between past and future, we find our place in time when we think, that is, when we are sufficiently removed from past and future to be relied on to find out their meaning, to assume the position of "umpire," of arbiter and judge over the manifold, never-ending affairs of human existence in the world. . . .

> And what is the "position of umpire," the desire for which prompts the dream, but the seat of Pythagoras' spectators, who are "the best" because they do not participate in the struggle for fame and gain, are disinterested, uncommitted, undisturbed, intent only on the spectacle itself? It is they who can find out its meaning and judge the performance.[135]

This place of judgment "between past and future" is, as Arendt herself indicates , identical to Nietzsche's gateway inscribed with the name "Moment."

Why is the gateway named "Moment"? Because it has no purpose outside itself, it leads to nothing but itself. Being is circular. Therefore, nothing outside the moment can serve to justify it; it alone can justify itself. It is, in Kantian terms, autonomous, an end-in-itself. Affirmation of the moment is possible only by reference to itself, not by reference to anything outside itself, for in the last analysis the ultimate conclusion or result of this moment is its own recurrence. The meaninglessness of temporal succession (and therefore of all Being, regarded as a temporal succession) is the hard truth that must be faced, according to Nietzsche, in bearing up under "the greatest stress." The circle is the symbol of pointlessness and futility; therefore, if the moment is to be affirmed, it shall have nothing to support it but itself. That is the meaning of the eternal return: for purposes of existential affirmation, the moment stands entirely on its own; it leads nowhere (since it leads back merely to itself), nor is it, itself, the culmination of a teleological sequence. How is it redeemable, how can it be affirmed? For Nietzsche the will, the iron resolve, to *think* this problem is itself its own solution. Those who can bear to *think* this problem in all its starkness will be the new creators, the redeemers of Western decadence. Arendt seeks elsewhere for a solution to what amounts to the same problem.

For Nietzsche, in common with Arendt, mastery of the problem of meaning depends on the possibility of establishing a genuine relation to the past. The problem, as Nietzsche sees it, is that failure to come to terms with the intractability of time gives rise to *revenge;* social-political ills stem from ontological frustration: "That time does not run backwards, that is [the will's] wrath; 'that which was' is the name of the stone he cannot move. . . . [The will] wreaks revenge for his inability to go backwards. This, indeed this alone, is what *revenge* is: the will's ill will against time and its 'it was.'"[136] To allow the will to feel a "good will" toward time would liberate man from revenge and thus revolutionize his entire social-political existence:

> To redeem those who lived in the past and to recreate all "it was" into a "thus I willed it"—that alone should I call redemption. Will—that is the name of the liberator and joybringer; thus I taught you, my friends. But now learn this too: the will itself is still a prisoner. Willing liberates; but what is it that puts even the liberator himself in fetters? "It was"—that is the name of the will's gnashing of teeth and most secret melancholy. Powerless against what has been done, *he is an angry spectator of all that is past.* The will cannot will backwards; and that he cannot break time and time's covetousness, that is the will's loneliest melancholy.[137]

Arendt's concern is not with liberation of the will but with liberation of the faculty of judgment, which, she says, takes place through exercise of the faculty of thinking. But the problem both she and Nietzsche confront is in this crucial respect the same: How can "an angry spectator" of the past be turned into a satisfied spectator? How can melancholy spectatorship be converted into happy spectatorship? Nietzsche wants to make the will contented with the past; Arendt seeks to make judging the past a source of pleasure rather than displeasure. In both cases, "a good will" toward time is to redeem the past.

Just as it may be said that Arendt initially sought a solution to the problem of "the moment" in the nature of acting and thus in some sense in willing (since there can be no action without the will) but that her ultimate solution reposes in reflective judgment or judging reflection upon the deeds of the past, so it is likewise possible to say that Nietzsche initially sought a solution to the problem of meaning (or nihilism, the devaluing of the highest values) in the will but that his ultimate solution, the thinking of the thought of the eternal return, leads away from the will. It is in precisely these terms that Arendt interprets Nietzsche's thought in chapter 14 of *Willing*. Eternal return "is not a theory, not a doctrine, not even a hypothesis, but a mere thought-experiment. As such, since it implies an experimental return to the ancient cyclical time concept, it seems to be in flagrant contradiction with any possible notion of the Will, whose projects always assume rectilinear time and a future that is unknown and therefore open to change."[138] Thus Arendt argues that the thought-experiment of the eternal return leads eventually to a "repudiation of the Will":

> the Will's impotence persuades men to prefer looking backward, remembering and thinking, because, to the backward glance, everything that is *appears* to be necessary. The repudiation of willing liberates man from a responsibility that would be unbearable if nothing that was done could be undone. In any case, it was probably the Will's clash with the past that made Nietzsche experiment with Eternal Recurrence.[139]

According to Arendt, Nietzsche

> embarked on a construction of the given world that would make sense, be a fitting abode for a creature whose "strength of will [is great enough] to do without meaning in things, . . . [who] can endure to live in a meaningless world." "Eternal Recurrence" is the term for this final redeeming thought inasmuch as it proclaims the *Innocence* of all Becoming" (*die Unschuld des Werdens*) and with that its inherent aimlessness and purposelessness, its freedom from guilt and responsibility.[140]

Eternal return is the means of coping with a meaningless world, reconciling oneself to it, redeeming it, by doing away with all concepts of responsibility, purposiveness, causality, will.

It is by the following argument that Nietzsche arrives at "the thought that everything that passes returns, that is, a cyclical time construct that makes Being swing within itself":

> If the motion of the world aimed at a final state, that state would have been reached. The sole fundamental fact, however, is that it does not aim at a final state; and every philosophy and scientific hypothesis (e.g., mechanistic theory) which necessitates such a final state is *refuted* [Nietzsche's italics] by this fundamental fact.
>
> I seek a conception of the world that takes this fact into account. Becoming must be explained without recourse to final intentions; *becoming must appear justified at every moment* (or incapable of being evaluated; which amounts to the same thing); *the present must absolutely not be justified by reference to a future, nor the past by reference to the present.*[141]

As must now be evident, this Nietzschean formulation is absolutely decisive for a proper appreciation of Arendt's statement of the problem of the "backward glance" of judgment. There can no longer be any mistaking her reliance on Nietzsche's way of posing the issue. In the same aphorism, Nietzsche writes: "Becoming is of equivalent value every moment."[142] In other words, no moment can serve to justify any other moment, no moment can be affirmed by reference to other moments; the moment must be self-redeeming. Arendt concludes from the passage just quoted that this "clearly spells a repudiation of the Will and the willing ego," because both presuppose the obsolete concepts of causality, intention, goal, etc.[143]

Nietzsche seeks for a way to eternalize the moment (" . . . joy wants eternity. Joy wants the eternity of *all* things, *wants deep, wants deep eternity*").[144] Arendt seeks for a way to immortalize the moment by an act of retrospective judgment. In both cases the impulse is the same: to save the moment from the fleeting onrush of time. Judging is able to perform this function by virtue of its essential *particularism,* the fact that it addresses itself to *particulars* without letting the particular be in any way reduced to, be swallowed up in, universals or generalities. The particular has a dignity of its own, one that no universal or generality can take from it.

Hegel is entirely right that philosophy, like the owl of Minerva, spreads its wings only when the day is over, at dusk. The same is not true for the beautiful or for any deed in itself. The beautiful is, in Kantian terms, an end in itself because all its possible meaning is contained within itself, without reference to others—without linkage, as it were, to other beautiful things. In Kant himself there is this contradiction: Infinite Progress is the law of the human species; at the same time, man's dignity demands that he be seen (every single one of us) in his particularity and, as such, be seen—but without any comparison and independent of time—as reflecting mankind in general.[145]

When looked at in the Nietzschean context, it becomes clear that, for Arendt, judging is not simply a capacity of political beings (although that was what originally prompted her to reflect on the faculty of judgment). It actually comes to serve an ontological function. (This is the insight lying behind the "break" between what I have called Arendt's early and late theories of judgment, the former "political," the latter "contemplative.") That is, judgment has the function of anchoring man in a world that would otherwise be without meaning and existential reality: a world unjudged would have no human import for us.

The parallel with Nietzsche—specifically, the fact that a confrontation with the problem of the will forced him to repudiate the will in favor of an affirmative acceptance of the eternal return, a nonvolitional reconciliation with all that is, was, and will be (again)—helps to shed light on the last sentences of Arendt's last work, *Willing* (which would otherwise appear quite baffling). After speaking of Augustine's discovery of human *natality*, "the fact that human beings, new men, again and again appear in the world by virtue of birth," Arendt observes that the Augustinian version of the argument

> seems to tell us no more than that we are *doomed* to be free by virtue of being born, no matter whether we like freedom or abhor its arbitrariness, are "pleased" with it or prefer to escape its awesome responsibility by electing some form of fatalism. This impasse, if such it is, cannot be opened or solved except by an appeal to another mental faculty, no less mysterious than the faculty of beginning, the faculty of Judgment, an analysis of which at least may tell us what is involved in our pleasures and displeasures.[146]

This passage confirms that her examination of judging was to be not merely a theoretical account of an important human capacity but, rather, the "solution" to an "impasse." The problem she was seeking to solve is how to be "pleased" with human freedom, how to bear "its awesome responsibility," how to avoid fatalism (which was the way out chosen by Nietzsche). The whole passage carries unmistakable echoes of (it reads like a kind of gloss on) the story in which Nietzsche describes "the greatest stress." If these speculations of mine have not been merely fanciful, this convergence is not at all fortuitous, for the path of reflection that led Arendt to consider the faculty of judging runs parallel to that which led Nietzsche to posit the eternal return. Indeed, *how else* could one explain Arendt's describing judgment as the way out of an impasse—in particular, the impasse of the will—or as a solution to the problem of affirming human freedom? Why should *this* be the way of introducing an analysis of judging? Why should *this* impasse be the one for which judging is looked to as a possible way out? And why should one contemplate *judgment* as a possible release from such an impasse? In the face of these questions, it seems fair to ask: On what other reading could one conceivably make sense of the final paragraph of Arendt's final work? Judgment is what keeps one from being crushed by the opposing forces of past and future while standing in "this gateway, Moment."

When one bears in mind the temporal direction of each of the three mental faculties, it is understandable why Arendt looked to judging, which is directed to the past, as the only possible way out of the impasse. The world we presently inhabit offers precious little prospect for genuine action and, therefore, for freedom. And the future, if anything, holds even less promise: "It is quite conceivable that the modern age—which began with such an unprecedented and promising outburst of human activity—may end in the deadliest, most sterile passivity history has ever known."[147]

Thus there is only the remotest possibility of deriving a sense of meaning from action in the present. (In these circumstances—in a world where the possibility of acting politically is more or less foreclosed—judging almost becomes a kind of vicarious action, a way of recouping our citizenship in default of a genuine public realm.) Nor is there any more reason to expect meaningfulness to be secured by willing projects or by projecting our will into the future (hence the impasse with respect to willing). That leaves the faculty of judgment, which can at least locate past events that redeem human existence. (As for thinking: according to Arendt it is the mental faculty by which we withdraw from the world of appearances; consequently, it cannot be a source of meaning for that world. Thinking, insofar as it returns to the world of appearances to reflect on particulars within it, becomes judging.) We can sustain ourselves in the present and retain hope for the future only by reflecting on the miraculousness of human freedom as instantiated in particular moments of the past. Without the possibility of retrospective judgment, we might well be overcome by a sense of the meaninglessness of the present and succumb to despair over the future. Judging alone makes satisfactory provision for meaning and thereby allows us, potentially, to *affirm* our condition.

Study of the "stories" of the historical past teach us that there is always the possibility of a new beginning; thus hope is latent in the very nature of human action. Every story has a beginning and an end—but never an absolute end; for the ending of one story always marks the beginning of another.[148] If we were compelled to pronounce an absolute verdict on history as a whole, we might be tempted to defer to Kant's pessimism. (It was precisely Kant's pessimism, combined with his conviction that human history must form a single story, that forced him to posit the regulative idea of historical progress, to guide our reflection as in teleological judgment, to make it possible for us to reflect on history without despair.) But because judging is always restricted to particular incidents and individuals, to stories that inspire us and examples that become exemplary, historical reflection will always remain edifying for those who have not relinquished hope.

We have argued that judging provides for affirmation of our worldly condition by allowing us to draw pleasure from reflecting on the past. But the aim is not really to justify the world but something more like "confirming" our place in it; that is, establishing contact with the reality of our world or, perhaps, justifying this reality by asserting our connection to it. This formulation is suggested by a phrase that recurs several times in Arendt's unpublished lectures; it is Augustine's "Amo: Volo ut sis": to love is, in effect, to say "I want you to be." Because of "the sheer arbitrariness of being," because of the fact that "we have not made ourselves," we "stand in need of confirmation. We are strangers, we stand in need of being welcome." It is by judging that "we confirm the world and ourselves"; with the faculties given us, "we make ourselves at home in the world."[149] The self-chosen company of shared judgment secures an otherwise tenuous historicity.

In these concluding speculations, I have not tried to dictate the necessary course of Arendt's reflections on judging; my intent has been merely to delimit the zone within which they circulate. This region of speculation is demarcated by Augustine's meditations on temporality in Book 11 of *The Confessions* and by Nietzsche's vision of the eternal return. Throughout her work Arendt is guided not only by Kant but also by Augustine and Nietzsche; again and again it is from them that she takes her problems. In the present context, the question they raise for her is this: Can the world be made a fitting abode for man, and in what sense, given that he is an essentially temporal being who enters from an unknown past and departs again into an unknown future?[150] Combining an Augustinian appreciation of the frailty of worldly institutions and relationships with a Nietzschean faith in the transfiguring potental of human action, Arendt confronts the basic question of temporality: Under what conditions can we say yes to time?[151] As posed either by Augustine or by Nietzsche, the problem—which haunts all of Arendt's philosophical work—is how to subdue temporality, how to consolidate and stabilize a mortal existence, rendering it less fleeting, ontologically less insecure. If the being of politics is indeed appearance (which is, after all, the fundamental premise of Arendt's political philosophy),[152] a public space of judgment is needed to render the world of appearances more durable—to confirm its being, as it were. Judging, or the saving power of remembrance, helps us to preserve what would otherwise be lost to time; it lets endure what is essentially perishable.[153] In other words, the ultimate function of judgment is to reconcile time and worldliness.

These speculations of mine no doubt raise more questions than they answer. The Kant Lectures certainly offer no more than an intimation of the possibilities I have suggested, and perhaps I have wandered farther than was called for. My only purpose has been to indicate the scope of Arendt's theorizing. Something of this scope is suggested by the themes and preoccupations we find in the hermeneutics of Hannah Arendt's friend Walter Benjamin, and it is by reading her alongside Benjamin's "Theses on the Philosophy of History" that we may finally hope to measure the dimensions of her intention. For Benjamin too sought for a redemptive relation to the past, and Arendt's judging spectator is the counterpart of Benjamin's *flâneur*, who strolls through the past, gathering moments in happy or melancholy retrospection, collecting by "re-collecting": amidst the ruin of the present, one searches out fragments by which to salvage one's past.[154] In Benjamin himself, this involves assuming the role of the angel of history, who, as Scholem puts it, is "basically a melancholy figure, wrecked by the immanence of history."[155] These themes converge in Benjamin's third thesis on the philosophy of history:

> A chronicler who recites events without distinguishing between major and minor ones acts in accordance with the following truth: nothing that has ever happened should be regarded as lost for history. To be sure, only a redeemed mankind receives the fullness of its past—which is to say, only for a redeemed mankind has its past become citable in all its moments. Each moment it has lived becomes a *citation à l'ordre du jour*—and that day is Judgment Day.[156]

Such a comportment toward the past is expressed even more tellingly in Benjamin's commentary on one of Kafka's parables:

> ...the true measure of life is memory. Looking back, it traverses the whole of life like lightning. As fast as one can turn back a few pages, it has travelled from the next village to the place where the traveller took the decision to set out. Those for whom life has become transformed into writing...can only read the writing backwards. That is the only way in which they confront themselves, and only thus—by fleeing from the present—can they understand life.[157]

Notes

Postscriptum to Thinking

1. Henri Bergson, *Time and Free Will,* trans. F. L. Pogson (New York: Macmillan, 1910), pp. 158, 167, 240 (italics added).
2. *Critique of Pure Reason,* B172–B173, trans. N. K. Smith (New York: St. Martin's Press, 1963).
3. [See Arendt's essay "The Concept of History: Ancient and Modern" in *Between Past and Future* (New York: Viking Press, 1968).—Ed.]

Kant Lectures

1. Hans Saner, *Kants Weg vom Krieg zum Frieden,* vol. 1: *Widerstreit und Einheit: Wege zu Kants politischem Denken* (Munich: R. Piper Verlag, 1967); English translation by E. B. Ashton, *Kant's Political Thought: Its Origin and Development* (Chicago: University of Chicago Press, 1973).
2. [I presume that this refers to *La Philosophie Politique de Kant,* volume 4 of the Annales de Philosophie Politique (Paris: Institut International de Philosophie Politique, 1962).—Ed.]
3. Immanuel Kant, *On History,* ed. Lewis White Beck, trans. L. W. Beck, R. E. Anchor, and E. L. Fackenheim, Library of Liberal Arts (Indianapolis: Bobbs-Merrill, 1963).
4. *Kant's Political Writings,* ed. Hans Reiss, trans. H. B. Nisbet (Cambridge, Eng.: At the University Press, 1971).
5. Kurt Borries, *Kant als Politiker: Zur Staats- und Gesellschaftslehre des Kritizismus* (Leipzig, 1928).
6. Kant, *On History,* ed. Beck, p. 75 ("The End of All Things"), and p. 54 ("Conjectural Beginning of Human History").
7. Ibid., p. 25 ("Idea for a Universal History," Ninth Thesis).
8. Ibid., p. 59 ("Conjectural Beginning of Human History").
9. *Critique of Judgment,* § 83. [As a rule, Arendt relies on the Norman Kemp Smith translation for the *Critique of Pure Reason* (New York: St. Martin's Press, 1963) and on the J. H. Bernard translation for the *Critique of Judgment* (New York: Hafner, 1951). But in her use of these,

as well as other translations, she commonly makes small changes of her own. In the case of other works, when translations are not specifically attributed, it may be assumed that they are Arendt's own.—Ed.]

10. *On History,* ed. Beck, p. 60 ("Conjectural Beginning of Human History").

11. Ibid., p. 54.

12. Ibid., pp. 78–79 ("The End of All Things").

13. Immanuel Kant, *Observations on the Feeling of the Beautiful and Sublime,* trans. John T. Goldthwait (Berkeley: University of California Press, 1960).

14. Letter to Christian Garve, September 21, 1798. See Kant, *Philosophical Correspondence 1759–99,* ed. and trans. Arnulf Zweig (Chicago: University of Chicago Press, 1967), p. 252.

15. Letters to Marcus Herz, November 24, 1776, and August 20, 1777. See *Philosophical Correspondence 1759–99,* ed. Zweig, pp. 86, 89.

16. See Lewis White Beck, *A Commentary on Kant's Critique of Practical Reason* (Chicago: University of Chicago Press, 1960), p. 6.

17. Immanuel Kant, "Reflexionen zur Anthropologie," no. 763 (italics added). In *Kants gesammelte Schriften,* Prussian Academy edition, 29 vols. (Berlin: Reimer & de Gruyter, 1902–83), 15:333.

18. *Observations on the Feeling of the Beautiful and the Sublime,* trans. Goldthwait, pp. 48–49 (note).

19. A. Baeumler, *Kants Kritik der Urteilskraft: Ihre Geschichte und Systematik,* vol. 1: *Das Irrationalitätsproblem in der Aesthetik und Logik des 18. Jahrhunderts bis zur Kritik der Urteilskraft* (Halle: Max Niemeyer Verlag, 1923), p. 15.

20. Immanuel Kant, *Logic,* trans. R. Hartman and W. Schwarz, Library of Liberal Arts (Indianapolis: Bobbs-Merrill, 1974), p. 29. [Arendt refers to Kant's *Vorlesungen über die Metaphysik.*]

21. Gottfried von Leibniz, "Principes de la Nature et de la Grâce, fondés en raison" (1714), par. 7.

22. *Critique of Judgment,* § 67.

23. Martin Heidegger, *Being and Time,* trans. John Macquarrie and Edward Robinson (New York and Evanston: Harper & Row, 1962), e.g., § 4.

24. See Gerhard Lehmann, *Kants Nachlasswerk und die Kritik der Urteilskraft* (Berlin, 1939), pp. 73–74.

25. *Critique of Judgment,* § 67.

26. Ibid., § 76.

27. Ibid., § 77.

28. Ibid., § 78.

29. Ibid., Preface.

30. Kant, Introduction to *The Metaphysics of Morals,* section I: "Of the Relation of the Faculties of the Human Mind to the Moral Laws". See *Kant's Critique of Practical Reason and Other Works on the Theory of Ethics,*

trans. Thomas Kingsmill Abbott (London: Longmans, Green, & Co., 1898), p. 267.

31. Ibid.

32. *On History*, ed. Beck, p. 102 (*Perpetual Peace*).

33. Ibid., p. 106.

34. Ibid., pp. 151–52, note (*The Strife of the Faculties*, Part II: "An Old Question Raised Again: Is the Human Race Constantly Progressing?").

35. Ibid., pp. 112–13 (*Perpetual Peace*).

36. Ibid., p. 112.

37. Kant, *Fundamental Principles of the Metaphysics of Morals*, trans. Thomas K. Abbott, Library of Liberal Arts (Indianapolis: Bobbs-Merrill, 1949), p. 19.

38. Ibid., pp. 20–21.

39. *Observations on the Feeling of the Beautiful and Sublime*, (end of Section Two), trans. Goldthwait, p. 74.

40. Ibid.

41. *On History*, ed. Beck, p. 145, note ("An Old Question Raised Again").

42. Aristotle, *Politics* 1267a10 ff.

43. Ibid., 1325b15 ff.

44. Blaise Pascal, *Pensées*, no. 331, trans. W. F. Trotter (New York: E. P. Dutton, 1958).

45. Robert D. Cumming, *Human Nature and History: A Study of the Development of Liberal Political Thought* (Chicago: University of Chicago Press, 1969), vol. 2, p. 16.

46. *Phaedo* 64.

47. Ibid. 67.

48. *Apology* 40.

49. *On History*, ed. Beck, p. 67 ("Conjectural Beginning of Human History").

50. *Critique of Judgment*, § 83 (note).

51. Kant, "Über das Misslingen aller philosophischen Versuche in der Theodicee" (1791), in *Gesammelte Schriften*, Prussian Academy edition, 8:253–71.

52. *Anthropology from a Pragmatic Point of View*, § 29, trans. Mary J. Gregor (The Hague: Nijhoff, 1974).

53. *Gesammelte Schriften*, Prussian Academy ed., 18:11.

54. *Critique of Pure Reason*, B839.

55. *Observations on the Feeling of the Beautiful and Sublime*, trans. Goldthwait, pp. 66–67.

56. *Critique of Judgment*, § 84 (italics added).

57. Kant, *Allgemeine Naturgeschichte und Theorie des Himmels* (1755), Appendix to Part III, *Gesammelte Schriften*, Prussian Academy ed., 1:357.

58. *Critique of Pure Reason*, B859.

59. Ibid., B884 (italics added).

60. "Bemerkungen zu den Beobachtungen über das Gefühl des Schönen und Erhabenen," *Gesammelte Schriften,* Prussian Academy ed., 20:44.

61. Aristotle's epistle to Alexander, "Concerning Kingship," in Ernest Barker, *The Politics of Aristotle* (Oxford: Oxford University Press, 1958), p. 386.

62. Eric Weil, "Kant et le problème de la politique," in *La Philosophie Politique de Kant,* vol. 4 of *Annales de Philosophie Politique* (Paris, 1962), p. 32.

63. "Reflexionen zur Logik," no. 1820a, *Gesammelte Schriften,* Prussian Academy ed., 16:127.

64. Kant, "Versuch einiger Betrachtungen über den Optimismus" (1759), in *Gesammelte Schriften,* Prussian Academy ed., 2:27–35.

65. *On History,* ed. Beck, pp. 73–74, note ("The End of All Things").

66. "Reflexionen zur Anthropologie," no. 890, *Gesammelte Schriften,* Prussian Academy ed., 15:388.

67. Karl Jaspers, *Kant,* ed. H. Arendt (New York: Harcourt, Brace & World, 1962), p. 95. (Jaspers quotes Kant without furnishing a reference, but see *Critique of Pure Reason,* B823.)

68. *Critique of Judgment,* § 40 (note).

69. *Critique of Pure Reason,* Axi, note (Preface to the first edition).

70. Ibid., B27.

71. Ibid., B370.

72. Ibid., Axii.

73. Ibid., Axi.

74. Ibid., Bxxv.

75. Ibid., Bxxxii.

76. Ibid., Bxxxiii.

77. Ibid., Bxxxv.

78. G. W. F. Hegel, "Über das Wesen der philosophischen Kritik" (1802), in *Sämtliche Werke,* ed. Hermann Glockner (Stuttgart, 1958), vol. 1, p. 185 [Arendt's translation].

79. Hegel, "Verhältniss des Skepticismus zur Philosophie" (1802), ibid., p. 243 [Arendt's translation].

80. See Kant's Preface to his essay "On the Common Saying: 'This May be True in Theory, but it does not Apply in Practice,'" in *Kant's Political Writings,* ed. Reiss, p. 61.

81. *Critique of Pure Reason,* Bxxxi.

82. Ibid., Bxxxvi.

83. *Theaetetus* 148 ff.

84. *Sophist* 226–31.

85. *Critique of Judgment,* § 40.

86. See *Gorgias* 482c.

87. *Critique of Pure Reason,* B884.

88. [Arendt's italics. See Kant, *Philosophical Correspondence 1759–99,* ed. Zweig, pp. 105–6.]

89. Jaspers, *Kant*, p. 123. The quote is from Kant's letter to Christian Garve, August 7, 1783.

90. *On History*, ed. Beck, pp. 4–5 ("What Is Enlightenment?").

91. Ibid., p. 5.

92. "Reflexionen zur Anthropologie," no. 897, *Gesammelte Schriften*, Prussian Academy ed., 15:392.

93. *Kant's Political Writings*, ed. Reiss, pp. 85–86 ("Theory and Practice").

94. "Was heisst: Sich im Denken orientieren?" (1786), in *Gesammelte Schriften*, Prussian Academy ed., 8:131–47.

95. *Gesammelte Schriften*, Prussian Academy ed., 18:267 (no. 5636).

96. Letter to Marcus Herz, June 7, 1771. See Kant, *Selected Pre-Critical Writings*, trans. G. B. Kerferd and D. E. Wolford (New York: Barnes & Noble, 1968), p. 108.

97. Letter to Marcus Herz, February 21, 1772. See Kant, *Philosophical Correspondence 1759–99*, ed. Zweig, p. 73.

98. *Critique of Judgment*, § 40.

99. Ibid.

100. *Gesammelte Schriften*, Prussian Academy ed., 12:59 (Correspondence).

101. *On History*, ed. Beck, pp. 143–48 ("An Old Question Raised Again," secs. 6 and 7).

102. *Kant's Political Writings*, ed. Reiss, p. 51 ("Idea for a General History from a Cosmopolitan Point of View," end of Eighth Thesis).

103. Ibid., p. 184, note (*The Contest of the Faculties*).

104. *On History*, ed. Beck, p. 120 (*Perpetual Peace*, Appendix I).

105. *Kant's Political Writings*, ed. Reiss, p. 147 (*The Metaphysics of Morals*, General Remark A after § 49).

106. *On History*, ed. Beck, p. 130 (*Perpetual Peace*, Appendix II).

107. See Borries, *Kant als Politiker* (Scientia Verlag Aalen, 1973; reprint of 1928 Leipzig edition), p. 16.

108. See Kant, *Religion within the Limits of Reason Alone*, Book IV, Part Two, §4, trans. T. M. Greene and H. H. Hudson (New York: Harper Torchbooks, 1960), pp. 176–77 (note).

109. *On History*, ed. Beck, pp. 129–30 (*Perpetual Peace*, Appendix II).

110. Ibid., p. 130.

111. Ibid., p. 133.

112. Ibid., p. 134.

113. [Arendt's translation from *Eine Vorlesung Kants über Ethik*, ed. Paul Menzer (Berlin: Pan Verlag Rolf Heise, 1924); see Kant, *Lectures on Ethics*, trans. Louis Infield (London: Methuen, 1979), p. 43 (section on "The Supreme Principle of Morality").]

114. *Kant's Political Writings*, ed. Reiss, p. 88 ("Theory and Practice," Part III).

115. See ibid., p. 116 (*Perpetual Peace*, Appendix I).

116. Ibid., p. 89 ("Theory and Practice," Part III).

117. Ibid., p. 91.

118. Ibid., p. 88.
119. *On History,* ed. Beck, p. 106 (*Perpetual Peace,* First Supplement).
120. Ibid., p. 100 (Second Definitive Article).
121. *Critique of Judgment,* §28.
122. *Kant's Political Writings,* ed. Reiss, p. 190 [the quote is actually borrowed from Hume].
123. *Critique of Judgment,* §83.
124. *Religion within the Limits of Reason Alone,* p. 29, note.
125. *Kant's Political Writings,* ed. Reiss, p. 174 (*The Metaphysics of Morals,* §62, Conclusion).
126. See *On History,* ed. Beck, p. 111 (the quote is from Seneca).
127. Diogenes Laertius, *Lives of the Philosophers* 8. 8, trans. G. S. Kirk and J. E. Raven, *The Presocratic Philosophers* (Cambridge, Eng.: At the University Press, 1971), p. 228.
128. See Hegel, *Reason in History,* trans. Robert S. Hartman, Library of Liberal Arts (Indianapolis: Bobbs-Merrill, 1953), pp. 35–36 (Hegel's Introduction to *The Philosophy of History*).
129. Alexandre Kojève, "Hegel, Marx and Christianity," *Interpretation* 1 (1970): 37.
130. *On History,* ed. Beck, p. 51 (Third Review of Herder).
131. Ibid.
132. *The Republic* 514a ff.
133. Introduction to *The Metaphysics of Morals,* section I (see n. 30, above).
134. *Critique of Pure Reason,* B825 ff.
135. Ibid., B883.
136. *Critique of Judgment,* §48.
137. Ibid., §50.
138. Ibid.
139. Ibid.
140. Ibid., §49.
141. Ibid.
142. Cicero, *On the Orator* 3. 195.
143. Ibid. 3. 197.
144. *Anthropology from a Pragmatic Point of View,* trans. Gregor, §53 (see n. 52, above).
145. *Critique of Judgment,* §40.
146. Parmenides (Frag. 4) speaks of *nous,* which enables us to look steadfastly at things that are present though they are absent: "Look how strongly absent things are present to the mind [*nous*]" (see Kathleen Freeman, *Ancilla to the Pre-Socratic Philosophers* [Oxford: Basil Blackwell, 1971], p. 42).
147. *Critique of Judgment,* §45.
148. Ibid., §41.
149. "Reflexionen zur Anthropologie," no. 767, in *Gesammelte Schriften,* Prussian Academy ed., 15:334–35.

150. *Critique of Judgment,* §48.
151. Ibid., §54.
152. *Anthropology from a Pragmatic Point of View,* trans. Gregor, §53.
153. *Critique of Judgment,* §40.
154. Ibid. See also Kant's *Logic,* trans. R. Hartman and W. Schwarz, p. 63 (see n. 20, above).
155. *Critique of Judgment,* §40. [On the translation of Kant's term *"allgemein":* it should be noted that Arendt consistently substitutes "general" where the standard translations have "universal." One important reason for this change is suggested in Arendt's essay "The Crisis in Culture" (in *Between Past and Future,* enl. ed. [New York: Viking Press, 1968], p. 221), where she says that "judgment is endowed with a certain specific validity but is never *universally* valid. Its claims to validity can never extend further than the others in whose place the judging person has put himself for his considerations. Judgment, Kant says, is valid 'for every single judging person,' but the emphasis in the sentence is on 'judging'; it is not valid for those who do not judge or for those who are not members of the public realm where the objects of judgment appear" (my italics). Thus Arendt's choice of terms here is of quite some importance in relation to her reading of Kant.—Ed.]
156. *Critique of Judgment,* §40.
157. Ibid.
158. Ibid., Preface.
159. Ibid., §41.
160. *On History,* ed. Beck, p. 54 ("Conjectural Beginning of Human History").
161. Cicero, *Tusculan Disputations* 1. 39–40.
162. *Critique of Judgment,* §41.
163. Ibid.
164. *On History,* ed. Beck, p. 89 (*Perpetual Peace*).
165. Ibid., p. 102.
166. Ibid., pp. 103, 105.
167. *Critique of Judgment,* Introduction, section IV.
168. Ibid.
169. *Critique of Pure Reason,* B173.

Imagination

1. Kant, *Critique of Pure Reason,* B151 (italics added), trans. N. K. Smith (New York: St. Martin's Press, 1963).
2. Kant, *Anthropology from a Pragmatic Point of View,* §28 (italics added), trans. Mary J. Gregor (The Hague: Nijhoff, 1974).
3. Ibid., §34.
4. See Kathleen Freeman, *Ancilla to the Pre-Socratic Philosophers* (Oxford: Basil Blackwell, 1971), p. 42.

5. Hermann Diels and Walther Kranz, *Die Fragmente der Vorsokratiker,* 5th ed. (Berlin), B21a. See Freeman, *Ancilla to the Pre-Socratic Philosophers,* p. 86.
6. *Critique of Pure Reason,* B176 ff.
7. Ibid., B103 (italics added).
8. Ibid., B180 (italics added).
9. Ibid., A124.
10. Ibid., B180.
11. Ibid., B29.
12. Ibid., B863.
13. Ibid., B180.
14. Ibid., A94.
15. Ibid., B180.
16. Ibid., B180–81.
17. Ibid., B181.
18. Ibid., A120 (note).
19. Ibid., B181.
20. Ibid., B104.
21. Ibid., A118.
22. *Critique of Judgment,* General Remark to §22, trans. J. H. Bernard (New York: Hafner, 1951).
23. Ibid., §59.
24. *Critique of Pure Reason,* B172.
25. Ibid., B173.
26. *Critique of Judgment,* §22.

Interpretive Essay

1. Hannah Arendt, *The Life of the Mind,* ed. Mary McCarthy (New York: Harcourt Brace Jovanovich, 1978), vol. 1: *Thinking,* p. 218 (Editor's Postface by Mary McCarthy).
2. J. Glenn Gray, "The Abyss of Freedom—and Hannah Arendt," in *Hannah Arendt: The Recovery of the Public World,* ed. Melvyn A. Hill (New York: St. Martin's Press, 1979), p. 225.
3. Michael Denneny, "The Privilege of Ourselves: Hannah Arendt on Judgment," in *Hannah Arendt: The Recovery of the Public World,* ed. Hill, p. 245.
4. *The Life of the Mind,* vol. 2: *Willing,* p. 217.
5. Arendt, Lectures on Kant's Political Philosophy (cited hereafter as Kant lectures), pp. 19, 30–31, above. (All page references to the Kant Lectures and to the *Postscriptum* to *Thinking* refer, unless otherwise stated, to the present volume.)
6. *Thinking,* pp. 69–70, 76, 92–98, 111, 129–30, 140, 192–93, 207–9, 213–16.
7. *Social Research* 38 (1971): 417–46.

8. See Kant Lectures, p. 68, above.

9. "*Postscriptum* to *Thinking*," p. 5, above; Kant Lectures, p. 56. Cf. "The Concept of History," in Hannah Arendt, *Between Past and Future: Eight Exercises in Political Thought,* enl. ed. (New York: Viking Press, 1968), pp. 41–90, esp. pp. 51–52; see also, ibid., pp. 262–63 ("Truth and Politics"). All references will be to the enlarged edition of *Between Past and Future.*

10. See section 8 of this essay, pp. 138–39, below.

11. Published, respectively, in *Freedom and Serfdom,* ed. A. Hunold (Dordrecht: D. Reidel, 1961), pp. 191–217; *Between Past and Future,* pp. 197–226; and ibid., pp. 227–64.

12. Mary McCarthy, Editor's Postface to *Thinking*, p. 219.

13. Arendt, "Understanding and Politics," *Partisan Review* 20 (1953): 377–92. Subsequent page references in the text are to this essay.

14. Preface to *Between Past and Future*, p. 14.

15. Arendt, "A Reporter at Large," *New Yorker*, February 16, 1963, pp. 40–113; February 23, 1963, pp. 40–111; March 2, 1963, pp. 40–91; March 9, 1963, pp. 48–131; March 16, 1963, pp. 58–134. See also Arendt, *Eichmann in Jerusalem: A Report on the Banality of Evil* (New York: Viking Press, 1963; rev. and enl. ed., 1965) (all references below are to the revised, enlarged edition). Although there are discussions of the faculty of judging in Arendt's writings prior to the Eichmann trial, the first version of the Kant Lectures was given in 1964, that is to say, immediately after the appearance of the Eichmann book.

16. See "Truth and Politics," *Between Past and Future*, p. 227 n.; "Thinking and Moral Considerations," *Social Research* 38 (1971): 417–19; *Thinking*, pp. 3–6. The promise of a book on "Thinking" emerges in 1964, in "Eichmann in Jerusalem" (*Encounter*, January, 1964, p. 56); Arendt wrote: "this is not the place to go into these matters seriously; I intend to elaborate them further in a different context. Eichmann may very well remain the concrete model of what I have to say."

17. *The Listener,* August 6, 1964, pp. 185–87, 205.

18. Ibid., p. 187.

19. *Eichmann in Jerusalem*, p. 294.

20. Ibid, pp. 294–95.

21. Ibid., p. 295.

22. *Encounter*, January, 1964, pp. 51–56. Reprinted in *The Jew as Pariah: Jewish Identity and Politics in the Modern Age*, ed. Ron H. Feldman (New York: Grove Press, 1978), pp. 240–51. This volume also contains a small selection of material relating to the Eichmann affair.

23. *Eichmann in Jerusalem*, pp. 295–96; my italics.

24. Ibid., p. 296.

25. Ibid.

26. Ibid., p. 297.

27. Ibid.

28. *The Jew as Pariah,* ed. Feldman, pp. 243, 248; my italics.
29. Maurice Merleau-Ponty, *Humanism and Terror,* trans. John O'Neill (Boston: Beacon Press, 1969), pp. xxiv–xxv; my italics.
30. "Freedom and Politics," in *Freedom and Serfdom: An Anthology of Western Thought,* ed. Hunold, p. 207. Cf. "The Crisis in Culture," *Between Past and Future,* pp. 219–20 (published in the same year).
31. Arendt, "The Crisis in Culture: Its Social and Its Political Significance," in *Between Past and Future,* pp. 197–226. Subsequent references in the text are to this work.
32. "By his manner of judging, the person discloses to an extent also himself, what kind of person he is, and this disclosure, which is involuntary, gains in validity to the degree that it has liberated itself from merely individual idiosyncrasies" (ibid., p. 223). In other words, even personal qualities are potentially nonsubjective, insofar as they establish the possibility of an intersubjectively valid "company" of like-judging persons.
33. Arendt here invokes Cicero's declaration that he would prefer to go astray with Plato than to possess the truth with the Pythagoreans, which she interprets as meaning that he would even accept being led astray from the truth for the sake of "Plato's company and the company of his thoughts" (ibid., pp. 224–25). In an unpublished lecture Arendt adds to this a similar statement by Meister Eckhart, that he would much rather be in Hell together with God than in Paradise without Him, and she also quotes *The Will to Power,* no. 292, where Nietzsche says that it is a denaturation of morality "to separate the act from the agent, to direct hatred or contempt against 'sin' [the deed instead of the doer], to believe that an action could be good or evil in itself. . . . In every action, all depends upon who does it, the same 'crime' may be in one case the highest privilege, and in another the stigma [of evil]. Actually, it is the self-relatedness of him who judges that interprets an action or rather its actor with respect to . . . resemblance or nonaffinity [between the agent and this judge]" (see Nietzsche, *The Will to Power,* ed. Walter Kaufmann, trans. W. Kaufmann and R. J. Hollingdale [New York: Random House, 1967], p. 165). This unpublished lecture was part of a lecture course Arendt gave at the New School for Social Research: "Some Questions of Moral Philosophy," Fourth Session, March 24, 1965 (Lecture notes, Hannah Arendt Papers, Library of Congress, Container 40, pp. 024637, 024651–024652); the interpolations in the Nietzsche quotation are Arendt's. Cf. Kant Lectures, p. 74, above. For further discussion of the concept "choice of company," see section 6 of this essay, pp. 112–14, below.
34. Arendt, "Truth and Politics," in *Between Past and Future,* pp. 227–64. Subsequent references in the text are to this work.
35. Lecture course at the New School: "Some Questions of Moral Philosophy," Fourth Session, March 24, 1965; also given as the final

lecture of "Basic Moral Propositions" at the University of Chicago (Hannah Arendt Papers, Library of Congress, Container 40, p. 024648).

36. Ibid.

37. Hannah Arendt, *On Revolution* (New York: Viking Press, 1965), p. 231.

38. Ibid., pp. 231–32.

39. *Thinking*, p. 192.

40. Ibid.

41. Arendt, "Thinking and Moral Considerations," *Social Research* 38 (1971):417–46.

42. Ibid., pp. 445–46. Cf. *Thinking*, pp. 192–93.

43. "The Concept of History," *Between Past and Future,* p. 52.

44. "The Crisis in Culture," *Between Past and Future,* p. 218.

45. Ibid., p. 210.

46. Ernst Vollrath, "Hannah Arendt and the Method of Political Thinking," *Social Research* 44 (1977): 163–64.

47. Arendt, "Thinking and Moral Considerations," p. 418.

48. For an explicit statement of method in connection with her work on totalitarianism, see Arendt's exchange with Eric Voegelin in "The Origins of Totalitarianism," *Review of Politics* 25 (1953): 68–85.

49. See "The Concept of History," *Between Past and Future,* p. 64.

50. Course at the New School: "Some Questions of Moral Philosophy," First Session (Hannah Arendt Papers, Library of Congress, Container 40, pp. 024585, 024583). See also Arendt, "Personal Responsibility under Dictatorship," *The Listener,* August 6, 1964, p. 205.

51. Course at Chicago: "Basic Moral Propositions," Seventeenth Session (Hannah Arendt Papers, Library of Congress, Container 41, p. 024560).

52. "Some Questions of Moral Philosophy," Fourth Session (Hannah Arendt Papers, Library of Congress, Container 40, p. 024651). See also "Eichmann in Jerusalem: An Exchange of Letters," *The Jew as Pariah,* p. 251, where Arendt says that, whereas thought tries to reach some depth, to go to the roots, "evil is never 'radical,' it is only extreme, and it possesses neither depth nor demonic dimension. It can overgrow and lay waste a world precisely because it spreads like a fungus on the surface. [The moment thought concerns itself with evil, it is frustrated because there is nothing.—R. B.] Only the good has depth and can be radical."

53. For a convincing illustration of Arendt's banality-of-evil thesis, see Henry T. Nash, "The Bureaucratization of Homicide," in *Protest and Survive,* ed. E. P. Thompson and Dan Smith (Harmondsworth: Penguin, 1980), pp. 62–74.

54. See section 2 of this essay; see also Arendt, "Tradition and the Modern Age," in *Between Past and Future,* pp. 17–40.

55. *Hannah Arendt: The Recovery of the Public World,* ed. Hill, pp. 311–15.

56. Arendt, "Thinking and Moral Considerations," p. 445; *Thinking,* p. 192.

57. J. Glenn Gray, "The Abyss of Freedom—and Hannah Arendt," in *Hannah Arendt: The Recovery of the Public World,* ed. Hill, p. 225.

58. *Willing,* p. 217. The quote from Augustine is from the *City of God* 12. 20.

59. *Postscriptum* to *Thinking,* p. 4, above.

60. Immanuel Kant, *Critique of Judgment,* trans. James Creed Meredith (Oxford: At the Clarendon Press, 1952), Introduction, sec. IV.

61. Ibid. Cf. Kant's *Logic,* trans. R. Hartman and W. Schwarz, Library of Liberal Arts (Indianapolis: Bobbs-Merrill, 1974), pp. 135–36, pars. 81–84.

62. Cf. the concepts of potential consensus and "ideal speech situation" in the recent work of Jürgen Habermas. Habermas himself actually acknowledges a considerable debt to Arendt's appropriation of Kant's idea of judging. See his "On the German-Jewish Heritage," *Telos* 44 (1980): 127–31, where he describes Arendt's "rediscovery of Kant's analysis of *Urteilskraft* or judgment for a theory of rationality" as an "achievement of fundamental importance" (p. 128). It is "a first approach to a concept of communicative rationality which is built into speech and action itself" and, as such, points in the direction of "a project of an ethics of communication which connects practical reason to the idea of a universal discourse" (pp. 130–31).

63. Arendt, "The Concept of History," *Between Past and Future,* p. 53.

64. Kant, *Anthropology from a Pragmatic Point of View,* trans. Mary Gregor (The Hague: Nijhoff, 1974), p. 12.

65. Cf. Stanley Cavell's essay "Aesthetic Problems of Modern Philosophy" in his book *Must We Mean What We Say?* (Cambridge, Eng.: At the University Press, 1976), pp. 73–96.

66. Edmund Burke, "On Taste: Introductory Discourse," *A Philosophical Enquiry into the Origin of Our Ideas of the Sublime and Beautiful,* in *The Writings and Speeches of Edmund Burke,* Beaconsfield edition, 12 vols. (London: Bickers & Son, n.d.), 1:79.

67. *Critique of Judgment,* § 19.

68. Ibid., §§ 20–22.

69. Ibid., § 22.

70. Kant, *On History,* ed. Lewis White Beck, trans. L. W. Beck, R. E. Anchor, and E. L. Fackenheim, Library of Liberal Arts (Indianapolis: Bobbs-Merrill, 1963), pp. 143–44 ("An Old Question Raised Again").

71. Ibid., pp. 145–46.

72. The philosophical historian draws attention to those world-historical phenomena that are "*not to be forgotten*" and thus are capable

of being "recalled on any favourable occasion by the nations which would then be roused to a repetition of new efforts of this kind" (ibid., p. 147)—precisely what Arendt herself does with her own historical study of revolutions!

73. Kant, *Observations on the Feeling of the Beautiful and Sublime*, trans. John T. Goldthwait (Berkeley: University of California Press, 1960), pp. 74–75.

74. See *Thinking*, p. 76, where Arendt says that judgment, "be it aesthetic or legal or moral, presupposes a definitely 'unnatural' and deliberate withdrawal from involvement and the partiality of immediate interests as they are given by my position in the world and the part I play in it." See also *Thinking*, chap. 11, "Thinking and Doing," pp. 92–97; and Kant Lectures, pp. 55 ff. On the conflict in Kant "between the principle according to which you should act and the principle according to which you judge" (Kant Lectures, p. 48), see Kant Lectures, p. 44, where Arendt says that the general standpoint of the spectator "does not tell one how *to act*," and also p. 53, where she remarks that the "insights of aesthetic and reflective judgment have no practical consequences for action." The comparison of thinking and judging in chapter 11 of *Thinking* makes clear Arendt's own position: although judging spectators do not share the solitude or self-sufficiency of philosophers, judgment, like thinking, presupposes withdrawal: "It does not leave the world of appearances but retires from active involvement in it to a privileged position in order to contemplate the whole" (*Thinking*, p. 94). The spectators are "disengaged from the particularity characteristic of the actor" (ibid.). This passage gives no indication that Arendt had any intention of trying to overcome the "clash between joint, participating action . . . and reflecting, observing judgment" (ibid., p. 95). She would, I think, have followed Kant in seeing action and judgment as governed by two distinct principles, which cannot be bridged.

75. Kant Lectures, pp. 61–62.

76. *Thinking*, pp. 95–96.

77. "On the Common Saying: 'This May be True in Theory, but it does not Apply in Practice,'" in *Kant's Political Writings*, ed. Hans Reiss (Cambridge, Eng.: At the University Press, 1970), p. 88.

78. *Anthropology from a Pragmatic Point of View*, trans. Gregor, p. 90.

79. Burke, "On Taste," *A Philosophical Enquiry*, in *Writings and Speeches of Edmund Burke*, Beaconsfield ed., vol. 1, p. 88.

80. *Observations on the Feeling of the Beautiful and the Sublime*, ed. Goldthwait, pp. 66–67.

81. Kant Lectures, p. 25, above.

82. Ibid., p. 77.

83. See *On Revolution*, pp. 265–66. To this list of examples, perhaps another may now be added: the Polish workers' revolt of 1980–81.

84. Ari Willner, Jewish Combat Group, Warsaw Ghetto, December, 1942 (quoted in an article by Leopold Unger in the *International Herald Tribune*).

85. Arendt, *The Human Condition* (Chicago: University of Chicago Press, 1958), pp. 5, 324–25; *Thinking*, p. 6.

86. For a persuasive critique of Arendt's interpretation of Kant on the autonomy of judging, see Barry Clarke, "Beyond 'The Banality of Evil,'" *British Journal of Political Science* 10 (1980): 417–39.

87. These three quotations are from *Thinking*, pp. 69, 70, and *Postscriptum* to *Thinking*, p. 4, above.

88. *Willing*, p. 217.

89. Kant Lectures, p. 13, above. Cf. *Hannah Arendt: The Recovery of the Public World*, ed. Hill, pp. 312–13.

90. Kant Lectures, p. 72; cf. p. 71.

91. Arendt, "What is Freedom?" in *Between Past and Future*, p. 152.

92. See *Thinking*, pp. 169–71: "The autonomy of mental activities . . . implies their being unconditioned. . . . Men, though they are totally conditioned existentially, . . . can mentally transcend all these conditions, but only mentally, never in reality, *or in cognition and knowledge*, by virtue of which they are able to explore the world's realness and their own" (my italics).

93. See ibid., chap. 20, and *Willing*, Introduction and chap. 6.

94. *Postscriptum* to *Thinking*, p. 5, above. On *Weltgericht*, see A. Kojève, "Hegel, Marx and Christianity," *Interpretation* I (1970): 36.

95. See Kant Lectures, pp. 76–77. Parenthetically, we may point out the implicit corollary to this view: namely, that Aristotle, with his account of practical judgment in the chapters on *phronēsis* in Book VI of the *Nicomachean Ethics*, is not a serious contender; only Hegel poses a credible challenge to Kant.

96. *Critique of Judgment*, § 40.

97. Ibid., § 19.

98. *Kant's Political Writings*, ed. Reiss, pp. 70–71, 73, 80, 86, 105, 122.

99. *Critique of Judgment*, Introduction, sec. I; *Foundations of the Metaphysics of Morals*, trans. Lewis White Beck, Library of Liberal Arts (Indianapolis: Bobbs-Merrill, 1959), pp. 33 ff.

100. See *Critique of Judgment*, § 53.

101. Ibid., §§ 13–14.

102. E.g., ibid., §§ 12, 40–41. Arendt never seriously considers what force is to be given to this "*a priori*," nor does she really confront the question of the nature of the judging community to which we are supposed to appeal (*a priori*). Arendt insists on translating Kant's "*allgemein*" as "general" rather than "universal" (see Notes to the Kant Lectures, note 155, p. 163, above); however, this still does not mean that we relate our judgment to any specifiable human community, with all the particularity that would entail.

103. *Critique of Judgment*, §40: we weigh our judgment, as it were, "with the collective reason of humanity" (*die gesammte Menschenvernunft*).
    104. In denying cognitive status to reflective judgment, Arendt is quite clearly following Kant, *Critique of Judgment*, §§ 1, 38 (Remark): "the judgment of taste is not a cognitive judgment."
    105. Jürgen Habermas, "Hannah Arendt's Communications Concept of Power," *Social Research* 44 (1977): 22–23.
    106. Kant *does* discuss such issues in his *Anthropology* (e.g., §§ 42–44). Perhaps an attempt to apply Kant's concept of taste to politics could derive more profit from the insights of Kant's "pragmatic anthropology," for there we find an account of taste considerably different from that elaborated in the third *Critique*. See *Anthropology from a Pragmatic Point of View*, §§ 67–71.
    107. "Some Questions of Moral Philosophy," Fourth Session (Hannah Arendt Papers, Library of Congress, Container 40, pp. 024642, 024645). The phrase I have italicized is a penciled-in addition to the typescript of the lecture.
    108. In his essay "Hannah Arendt's Communications Concept of Power" (p. 24), Jürgen Habermas concludes that Arendt "retreats" from "her own concept of a praxis, which is grounded in the rationality of practical judgment."
    109. Kant Lectures, p. 10, above.
    110. Arendt, "The Crisis in Culture," *Between Past and Future*, p. 221.
    111. *Thinking*, p. 40.
    112. Lecture course at Chicago on "Kant's Political Philosophy," Fall, 1964 (Hannah Arendt Papers, Library of Congress, Container 41, p. 032272).
    113. Ibid., p. 032259.
    114. See *Thinking*, pp. 236–37, n. 83: "my chief reservations about Kant's philosophy concern precisely his moral philosophy, that is, the *Critique of Practical Reason*." Arendt does not explore points of contact between the second and third *Critiques*, nor does she discuss the possibility that deficiencies in his moral philosophy are reproduced in his aesthetics and philosophy of politics.
    115. "Freedom and Politics," in *Freedom and Serfdom*, ed. Hunold, p. 207.
    116. Kant Lectures, p. 7, above.
    117. Ibid., pp. 31, 33.
    118. Ibid., pp. 9, 19.
    119. Martin Heidegger, *Kant and the Problem of Metaphysics*, trans. J. S. Churchill (Bloomington: Indiana University Press, 1962), p. xxv.
    120. *The Human Condition*, p. 235, n. 75.
    121. "Truth and Politics," *Between Past and Future*, p. 262. Cf. Arendt, "Isak Dinesen 1885–1963," *Men in Dark Times* (London: Cape, 1970), p. 107.

122. On hope, see Kant Lectures, pp. 46, 50, 54, 56.
123. Diogenes Laertius, *The Lives of Famous Philosophers* 8. 8. This passage, used as the epigraph to section 7 of this essay, is cited in *Thinking*, p. 93, and in the Kant Lectures, p. 55, above. Arendt also refers to it in the transcript of discussions "On Hannah Arendt" in *Hannah Arendt: The Recovery of the Public World*, ed. Hill, p. 304.
124. See *Thinking*, pp. 211–12.
125. Kant Lectures, p. 77.
126. Friedrich Nietzsche, *On the Genealogy of Morals*, 3. 28, in *Basic Writings of Nietzsche*, trans. and ed. Walter Kaufmann (New York: Modern Library, 1968), p. 598.
127. *Oedipus at Colonus*, lines 1224 ff.; *The Birth of Tragedy*, sec. 3, *Basic Writings of Nietzsche*, trans. and ed. Kaufmann, p. 42. See also Kant Lectures, p. 23.
128. *On Revolution*, p. 285.
129. Friedrich Nietzsche, *The Gay Science*, no. 341, in *The Portable Nietzsche*, trans. and ed. Walter Kaufmann (New York: Viking Press, 1968), pp. 101–2.
130. *Critique of Judgment*, § 83, note. Cf. Kant Lectures, p. 24.
131. *Thus Spoke Zarathustra*, Third Part: "On the Vision and the Riddle," *The Portable Nietzsche*, trans. and ed. Kaufmann, p. 270.
132. Ibid., pp. 269–70.
133. *Thinking*, p. 204.
134. Ibid., p. 207.
135. Ibid., pp. 207, 209.
136. *Thus Spoke Zarathustra*, Second Part: "On Redemption," *The Portable Nietzsche*, trans. and ed. Kaufman, pp. 251–52.
137. Ibid., p. 251; my italics.
138. *Willing*, p. 166.
139. Ibid., p. 168.
140. Ibid., p. 170.
141. *The Will to Power*, no. 708, ed. Kaufmann (see n. 33, above), p. 377 (my italics). Again, Nietzsche seems to echo a thought already present in Kant, who said, "It will always remain bewildering ... that the earlier generations seem to carry on their burdensome business only for the sake of the later ... and that only the last should have the good fortune to dwell in the [completed] building" ("Idea for a Universal History with a Cosmopolitan Purpose," Third Thesis; quoted by Arendt in "The Concept of History," *Between Past and Future*, p. 83).
142. *The Will to Power*, no. 708, ed. Kaufmann, p. 378.
143. *Willing*, p. 172.
144. *Thus Spoke Zarathustra*, Fourth Part: "The Drunken Song," sec. 11, *The Portable Nietzsche*, trans. and ed. Kaufmann, p. 436.
145. Kant Lectures, p. 77, above.
146. *Willing*, p. 217.
147. *The Human Condition*, p. 322.

148. See "Understanding and Politics," *Partisan Review* 20 (1953): 388–89.

149. Arendt's lecture course at Chicago, "Kant's Political Philosophy," Fall, 1964 (Hannah Arendt Papers, Library of Congress, Container 41, pp. 032288, 032295). The same phrase is also cited by her in "Basic Moral Propositions" (Container 41, p. 024560), where it is related to *dilectores mundi:* "the love of the world constitutes the world for me, fits me into it," in the sense that it determines "to whom and to what I belong." Cf. *Willing,* pp. 104, 144. See also the discussion of love in chapters 10–12 of *Willing.*

150. Cf. Augustine's *Confessions* 11. 14: Of the three divisions of time, "how can two, the past and the future, *be,* when the past no longer is and the future is not yet? As for the present, if it were always present and never moved on to become the past, it would not be time but eternity. If, therefore, the present is time only by reason of the fact that it moves on to become the past, how can we say that even the present *is,* when the reason why it *is* is that it is *not to be?* In other words, we cannot rightly say what time *is,* except by reason of its impending state of *not being.*" See also the meditation on mortality in *Confessions* 4. 4 ff.

151. "A certain emperor always bore in mind the transitoriness of all things so as not to take them too seriously and to live at peace among them. To me, on the contrary, everything seems far too valuable to be so fleeting: I seek an eternity for everything: ought one to pour the most precious salves and wines into the sea?—My consolation is that everything that has been is eternal: the sea will cast it up again" (Nietzsche, *The Will to Power,* no. 1065, ed. Kaufmann, pp. 547–48).

152. *The Human Condition,* p. 199.

153. See Arendt's essay, "The Crisis in Culture," in *Between Past and Future,* p. 218. The concern with "imperishability" actually goes back to Arendt's very first book, on Saint Augustine's concept of love, published in 1929. Her work on judging would thus have closed a circle of reflection dating back to the very start of her philosophical career.

154. See Walter Benjamin, "Theses on the Philosophy of History," in *Illuminations,* ed. H. Arendt, trans. Harry Zohn (New York: Harcourt, Brace & World, 1968), pp. 255–66. The idea of our fragmented relation to the past is expressed in Benjamin's concept of *Jetztzeit,* which he discusses in several of his theses. For example, in the fourteenth thesis Benjamin describes how Robespierre brought ancient Rome to life by blasting it out of the homogeneous continuum of history. The French Revolution "evoked ancient Rome the way fashion evokes costumes of the past" (p. 263). For Arendt's commentary on this aspect of Benjamin's thought, see her Introduction to *Illuminations,* pp. 38–39 and 50–51.

155. Gershom Scholem, *On Jews and Judaism in Crisis* (New York: Schocken, 1976), pp. 234–35. For Arendt's own commentary on Benjamin's ninth thesis on the philosophy of history, see *Illuminations,* ed.

Arendt, pp. 12–13. It would be impossible here to explore the many points of affinity between Arendt and Benjamin. Let us note merely that Arendt's appeal to Cato's image of the historian who sides with the defeated cause is in close accord with the spirit of Benjamin's seventh thesis. See Theodor Adorno, *Minima Moralia,* no. 98 (London: New Left Books, 1974), p. 151.

156. *Illuminations,* ed. Arendt, p. 256.

157. Walter Benjamin, "Conversations with Brecht," in Ernst Bloch et al., *Aesthetics and Politics* (London: New Left Books, 1977), p. 91. The story by Kafka, for which Benjamin offers this exegesis, is "The Next Village."